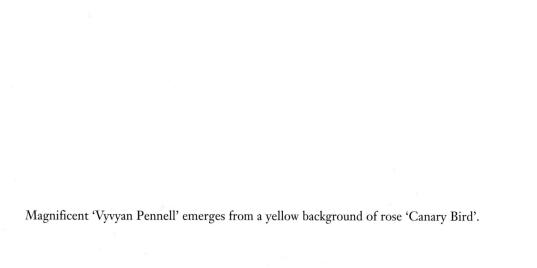

Magnificent 'Vyvyan Pennell' emerges from a yellow background of rose 'Canary Bird'.

The Rose *and* *the* Clematis
as good companions

Clematis 'Twilight' and Rose 'New Dawn'

Frontispiece: Clematis 'Marie Boisselot' with the Rose 'Compassion'.

The Rose *and the* Clematis

as good companions

Clematis 'General Sikorski' and Rose 'Graham Thomas'

John Howells

Photographs by the author
Flower arrangements by Ola Howells

GARDEN • ART • PRESS

ISBN 1 870673 19 0

British Library Cataloguing-in-Publication Data
A catalogue record for this book is available from
the British Library

Published by Garden Art Press,
a division of Antique Collectors' Club Ltd.

Printed in England
by the Antique Collectors' Club Ltd., Woodbridge, Suffolk, UK
on Consort Royal Satin paper supplied by the Donside Paper Company,
Aberdeen, Scotland

LIST OF CONTENTS

*Clematis 'Victoria' with the
Rose 'Casino'*

Rose 'Dame Wendy' grows happily with Clematis 'Perle d'Azur' to produce a colourful combination of blooms.

Clematis 'Perle d'Azur' and 'Viticella Rubra' produce a striking effect when grown against a wall.

ACKNOWLEDGEMENTS

Who, as a rosarian, should I, as a clematarian, consult on material about roses? Perhaps it should be as eminent a source as a Past President of the World Federation of Rose Societies, or a Past President of the Royal National Rose Society, or a Past Master of the Worshipful Company of Gardeners of London. In fact, I consulted all three in the person of Dick Balfour whose constructive comments have added to the value of the book and to the author's confidence. Mrs Natalie Finch gave generously of her knowledge of shrub roses. Garry Ravenhall gave invaluable advice on the intricacies of colour.

I must thank the many gardeners who have allowed me to photograph their plants, with special thanks to my plantsman friend, Lewis Hart of Hadleigh. Graham Hutchins of County Park Nursery in Hornchurch, Ruth Gooch of Thorncroft Nursery and Frank Cadge of Acton freely allowed me access to their stocks.

It is a pleasure to record the enjoyable collaboration with my publisher, Diana Steel of the Antique Collectors' Club and her team of Stephen Farrow, Sandra Pond and Peter Robertson. Diana's personal involvement in the book is manifest in her contribution of additional colour plates. I have been supported as always by the efficiency and exactitude of my Literary Assistant, Janet Hodge. My wife Ola made our partnership tangible with beautiful floral arrangements and two of our grandchildren, Anna and Julian, have been occasional eager and accurate photographic assistants.

English Rose 'Evelyn' blends effectively with clematis 'Ernest Markham'.

PLATE 1. The gardener may want to use Roses and Clematis to add to the vibrant colours of the garden as shown here, growing in Inverewe, Scotland.

INTRODUCTION

In nature plants are always in companionship. There is always a neighbouring plant, sometimes many. Of near neighbours, climbing roses and clematis are supreme companions, the king and queen of climbers. Both are extensively grown, especially roses, but notice how monotonous even the most beautiful climbing roses can look on their own. They need companions to relieve the monotony and, by contrast and harmony, bring out the wonderful beauty of the rose. This is an acknowledged modern requirement of a rosarium (a rose garden) as monotonous rigid displays are a thing of the past. The rose needs natural companions.

Climbing roses and clematis are natural companions. Both are climbers, reaching for the sun. In its quest upwards the clematis needs to cling and the rose gives that support. The support is informal, natural, with soft lines - unlike that given by a rigid trellis.

Not only do climbing roses and clematis share a movement upwards but they are alike in requiring the same growing conditions. Both require a rich soil – best given by good soil and an organic fertiliser. If boosting of nutriment is required then both can benefit from the same fertilisers. Both, especially clematis, need to be well watered and so each gains from the watering programme. It is to the advantage, too, of these companions to share the same mulch.

PLATE 2. A pergola can support a number of clematis and roses. To the left Viticella 'Minuet'. To the right find single blooms of pale violet 'Proteus' mingling with red 'Mme Edouard André', the whole supported by rose 'Compassion'.

A colourful scene, with the effective use of posts to support climbing roses, can be enhanced with the addition of clematis.

The main enemies of roses and clematis are again common to both. The fungal condition 'black spot' in roses is matched by the fungal condition of 'wilt' in clematis. Both will respond to the same agents. Some roses and clematis can be susceptible to mildew. Again, both readily respond to the same agents. Harmful insects on both plants respond to the same insecticides.

Roses are never blue. Clematis are often blue. Clematis are rarely yellow. Roses are often yellow. Here is the chance, by matching, to improve both rose and clematis to create a striking combination in the garden of blue clematis and yellow/orange roses.

The great majority of climbing roses and clematis plants are of a similar size with the result that neither swamps the other.

Fragrance is rare in large flowered clematis while it is common in roses. Here again they complement each other.

Not only can climbing roses and clematis be good companions but so can clematis and shrub roses and bedding roses – as we shall see.

CHAPTER ONE
Clematis and Roses as Garden Plants

HISTORY

Clematis

Most countries in the temperate regions of the northern hemisphere and, to a lesser extent, the southern hemisphere, have native clematis. There are over 250 wild native clematis - more even than roses. For example, southern Europe has *C. alpina* while the Mediterranean region has *C. cirrhosa*. India has the white and China the pink *C. montana* while Great Britain has *C. vitalba* (see Plate 3), Japan *C. patens*, South Africa *C. brachiata*, Australia *C. aristata*, New Zealand *C. afoliata* and the Americas have *C. virginiana*, among many others.

Plant hunters collected these native clematis to bring them back to enrich the flora of their own country. At first they went to nearby countries. For instance *C. viticella* was brought from Spain to England in 1569 and became a very important parent in hybridising efforts. In 1596 three more came from Europe to Great Britain - *C. flammula*, *C. cirrhosa* and *C. integrifolia*. These again were to be used in hybridising programmes so as to produce new varieties.

In the 19th Century plant hunters went further afield - especially to China and Japan. This led to a dramatic improvement in clematis and imports into Europe produced the large flowered varieties that we know today. Between 1860-1880 there was a revolution in the state of clematis with the first to hit the headlines being *C. jackmanii* named after the nursery in Woking, UK, where it was introduced in 1862. Later this nursery had a list of over 340 clematis in stock! In a

PLATE 3. The native clematis 'Vitalba' embellishes trees and shrubs with a coating of white bloom on the South Downs, United Kingdom.

PLATE 4. Clematis 'Perle d'Azur' was bred in France before 1885 and is the world's most popular clematis today.

recent survey, eight out of ten of the most popular clematis, including the world's sweetheart, 'Perle d'Azur' (see Plate 4), came from the nineteenth century.

About 1880, however, disaster struck. There was a maggot in the apple! These lovely plants developed a wilt condition named 'la maladie noir' by the French because of the blackening of the stem. Many theories were invented but it is only today that the malady is completely understood. In 1880, the impact was dramatic; the plant nurseries and the public lost interest in clematis – a position which continued until the 1950s.

After the Second World War, as nurseries began to pick up, they were able to use effective fungicides which had been unknown in the past. Also hybridists developed interesting worthwhile varieties out of the wild clematis. Hope returned. Hygiene improved in the nursery. Hybridising programmes produced outstanding new large flowered clematis, gardeners found ways of coping with the wilt and enthusiasm spread. In today's garden there is a massive return of interest in the clematis with the specialist clematis nurseries enjoying a boom. The clematis has come of age.

Roses

Throughout recorded history there has been mention of the rose. Many countries had their wild roses which were subsequently introduced into the garden with colours limited to white, pink and red (see Plate 5). They usually only flowered once but they had one enormous virtue - they had fragrance. These Old Roses were the Gallicas, Damasks, Albas and the Centifolias.

PLATE 5. 'Gloire de Dijon', a Noisette Climber, introduced in 1853, is still a fine Climbing Rose for use today.

PLATE 6. The hybridist is still at work developing roses. 'Graham Thomas', named after a famous rosarian, is a good example of the New English Rose.

Roses from China came into Europe at the beginning of the last century and these were ultimately to produce the Hybrid Tea roses through a long process of hybridising; the China roses brought in the capacity to repeat flowering which was invaluable. There was now a great variety of colours and wonderful shapes to the blooms although one ingredient was lacking, there was no orange and not much yellow bloom. By hybridising with Persian roses, orange and yellow were introduced to the Hybrid Teas but this was at a price, a vulnerability to 'black spot'.

A group of roses, the Polyantha Roses, was crossed with Hybrid Teas and produced a new type of Bedding Rose with clusters of flowers. These were termed the Floribundas. They had the capacity for continuous flowering blooms in clusters, a great variety of colour but, unhappily, little scent.

Such attention was given to shape and colour in developing the rose that the quality of fragrance was almost forgotten. One of the tasks for the modern hybridist has been to bring fragrance back to the Bedding Rose. A particular effort in this direction was the coming of the English Rose; the best of the Old Roses were combined with the New, bringing with them from the past two splendid qualities, shape and scent (see Plate 6). At least three English Roses can climb - 'Constance Spry', 'Francine Austin', and 'Shropshire Lass'.

Roses with a capacity to climb were not forgotten by the hybridist. The Rambler Roses were developed with clusters of bloom rather like the Floribundas, which they preceded, although these usually had only one burst of flowering in the spring. Contemporary hybridists are hard at work on this deficiency and soon there will be repeat flowering Ramblers - for example, 'Super Excelsa'. The counterpart of Hybrid Teas were the Climbing Roses which had larger blooms, often repeat flowering and many had scent. A fascinating recent innovation is the production of Miniature Climbing Roses.

In addition to the 19th century Shrub Roses, many have been developed in the 20th century which are larger than the Bedding Roses and tend to have fragrance. Most have only one blooming, although a few repeat and all have a strong constitution. The hybridising continues to improve modern Shrub Roses.

In the garden there have been changes of fashion in the use of the rose. In the Victorian period roses were seen largely as shrubs and wall plants. With the advent of the striking Hybrid Tea we had the development of rose beds. Today we are on the verge of another change where the taste is not for large blobs of colour but rather for the fusion of the colours of the rose with other plants. This book is about the combination of clematis and rose and the fusion of colour which this produces.

GROUPING

A knowledge of how the clematis and the rose plants are classified into distinctive groups adds greatly to the gardener's capacity to match the companions.

Clematis

The gardener needs to know the general characteristics of the various groups of clematis so that he can take the special qualities of each group into account when he plans his garden. Furthermore, if clematis are to be grown with roses then the same applies - the rosarian needs to know when the various groups of clematis flower, their height, habit, fragrance, colour, etc.

At one time clematis were grouped or classified according to their pruning requirements. While this was useful when pruning it told us nothing about the general characteristics of the clematis. In this book a new, more useful, and easily understood classification is employed.[1] We need to know this so that we can match the right clematis with the right rose at the right time.

Gardeners are frequently attracted to clematis by the sight of the dramatic,

1. Howells, J. **A Gardener's Classification of Clematis.** *The Clematis*, 1992, p.34

PLATE 7. 'Miss Bateman' of the Early Large Flowered Group has a dramatic coloured bloom. Flowering very early she displays an attractive tinge of green.

PLATE 8. 'Gipsy Queen' is a reliable member of the Late Large Flowered Clematis. This young bloom shows its velvety sheen.

eye-catching Large Flowering Clematis. Soon he discovers that there is an extensive, more fascinating, and as colourful group of Small Flowering Clematis. The Large Flowered were cultivars (gardener made) from crossings between the largest of the wild clematis that came from Japan and China while the Small Flowered are the wild clematis from many parts of the world and collected because they add beauty to our gardens; some of these have been developed to produce new hybrids.

So we have our first great division –

Division I – Large Flowered Clematis – cultivated.
Division II – Small Flowered Clematis – from the wild clematis.

There are twelve groups in all, two are Large Flowered and ten are Small Flowered.

There are some general differences between the two main divisions. The Large Flowered Clematis have lace-like roots, large flowers that are rarely scented and plants that can suffer from wilt. The Small Flowered Clematis, on the other hand, tend to have fibrous roots, have many small flowers, are often scented, are easy to grow and rarely suffer from wilt.

Both the Large and Small Flowered divisions can be sub-divided into groups.

The most useful grouping of the Large Flowered is into Early and Late Flowering. There is a reason for this grouping. The Early Large Flowered bloom on growth made the previous year, so naturally they need little pruning or the blooms will be pruned away. Examples would be 'Nelly Moser', 'Miss Bateman' (see Plate 7), 'General Sikorski', 'Dr Ruppel'. The Late Large Flowered, on the other hand, bloom on growth made in the present season so it makes sense to prune them severely in the early spring to encourage them in the production of strong growth for an abundance of flowers later. Examples would be 'Hagley Hybrid', 'Comtesse de Bouchaud', 'Jackmanii', 'Gipsy Queen' (see Plate 8), etc.

Another useful sub-division of the Large Flowered is to divide them up according to colour - white, pink, red, blue, by shape of flower - single or double, and whether they are striped or unstriped.

PLATE 9. The variety 'Apple Blossom' of *Clematis armandii* of the Evergreen Group produces a large display of clusters of beautiful pink and white blooms, gorgeously scented in late winter.

PLATE 10. *Clematis alpina* 'Frances Rivis' of the Alpina Group produces elegant, long dangling bells to bring colour in early spring.

In the Small Flowered Clematis there are many more groups - often very different from one another and with very distinct qualities. Again there are early flowering forms (needing no pruning) and late flowering forms (all needing severe pruning).

There are five groups in the Small Flowered early forms and these can be considered according to the order of their approximate time of flowering:

1. The first of the Small Flowered to bloom are those of the Evergreen Group. They flower from midwinter onward. Examples would be *Clematis cirrhosa* and *Clematis armandii* making very large plants (see Plate 9). They surprise everyone in winter with unexpected profuse flowering.

2. Next are the hardy Alpina Group. They make a selection of single multi-coloured bells from early spring on plants of medium height. Examples would be *C. alpina* 'Frances Rivis' (see Plate 10) and *C. alpina* 'Constance'.

3. The next Group, the Macropetala, bloom almost at the same time. Here we have not single but double nodding bells in a variety of colours from early spring onwards on plants of medium height. Examples would be 'Markham's Pink' (see Plate 11) and 'Rosy O'Grady'.

PLATE 11. 'Markham's Pink' of the Macropetala Group covers a substantial area with pink double bells in early spring.

PLATE 12. The Montana Group produces the giant plants of the clematis world. The variety 'Mayleen', seen here, easily climbs up and over a roof.

The Alpina and Macropetala Groups planted near a window, give the gardener a colourful vista in early spring. This can even be on the north side of the house. Both Groups are very resistant to low temperatures and can thus survive in very cold climates.

4. Next to make a dramatic entrance are plants of the Montana Group. Many, not aware of the beauties that have gone before, regard these as starting the clematis season. A plant can be huge, almost overpowering, and covered with thousands of blooms. Examples would be 'Mayleen' (see Plate 12) and 'Pink Perfection'.

5. While the above have been attracting attention, below them at almost ground level is the lovely Rockery Group. Hardly exploited as yet, in time this will be a popular group for the beauty of its delicate flowers. Examples would be *C. marmoraria* (see Plate 13) and *C. cartmanii* 'Joe'. Flowering from early spring onwards, it is good to have this display at a time of year when there is so little colour in the garden.

PLATE 13. In contrast to the Montanas the Rockery Group produces beauty in miniature. *C. marmoraria*, only a few cm. tall, is the smallest of all clematis.

PLATE 14. The Herbaceous Group is represented here by the beautiful hanging bells of *integrifolia* 'Rosea'.

In the Late Flowering forms we also have five groups, each very different from the next. Their flowering can overlap but they flower approximately in the following order:

1. The Herbaceous Group contains a number of wonderful plants for borders. They clamber over other plants rather than climb. Being herbaceous they lose their stems in the winter. Examples are *C. durandii* and *C. integrifolia* 'Rosea' (see Plate 14). They can flower from early summer onwards.

2. The Viticella Group is of outstanding merit and competes with the Large Flowered Group for garden worthiness. They tend to send out very strong stems, sometimes to a very great height, and are covered with a large number of medium sized flowers from midsummer onwards. They are trouble free, hardy, and have fascinating shapes and colours. Examples would be 'Mme Julia Correvon',

PLATE 15. The Viticella Group has plants of great attraction and diversity. 'Alba Luxurians' seen here has an unusual bloom as if unsure whether to produce leaves or tepals.

PLATE 16. The eye-catching elegant trumpets of the Texensis Group are represented here by the satiny multicoloured flower of 'Sir Trevor Lawrence'.

'Little Nell' and 'Alba Luxurians' (see Plate 15).

3. The Texensis Group of late summer again has distinctive qualities. Bushes of medium height tend to climb or clamber over other plants. The flowers are tulip- or trumpet-shaped with glowing colours. Each flower is of such beauty as to demand individual attention. Examples would be 'Sir Trevor Lawrence' (see Plate 16) and 'Etoile Rose'.

4. The Orientalis Group contains the truly yellow clematis. The yellows are vivid and make no apology for it. Fine seedheads are a feature of this group. Bushes are usually of medium height but some can be tall. They flower midsummer onwards but are more conspicuous in early autumn as colour disappears elsewhere in the garden. Examples are *C. tangutica* and *C. orientalis* 'Bill Mackenzie' (see Plate 17).

PLATE 17. The Orientalis Group brings yellow into the clematis world seen here in the open bell of the popular 'Bill Mackenzie'. The flower makes fine seed heads.

PLATE 18. The Late Species Group brings the clematis year to an end with a display of vigour, colour and scent. The small star-shaped blooms of *Clematis flammula* are produced in myriads to make a large bush emitting scent discernible metres away.

5. The Late Species Group brings the clematis year to an end in a burst of glory. Some of the plants are very vigorous as well as being scented. Examples would be *Clematis flammula* (see Plate 18) and *Clematis fargesii*.

To summarise, we have two main divisions:

    I Large Flowered (with two sub-groups)
      - Early and Late Flowering Clematis.
   II Small Flowered (with ten sub-groups)
      - Five Early and five Late Flowering Groups.

The range of clematis is probably much greater than the reader suspects. To know both Early and Late Groups of the Large Flowered, and to know all ten groups of the Small Flowered, twelve groups in all, will give you a wealth of choices to match your roses at different times of the year. Please read and re-read this section of the book until you are familiar with the choices before you. Time spent on this will greatly help you in the garden. Growing one clematis from each of the twelve groups will quickly show you their respective qualities.

The classification of clematis is summarised in Table I:

Table I
THE TWELVE CLEMATIS GROUPS

LARGE FLOWERED (TWO GROUPS)	SMALL FLOWERED (TEN SUB-GROUPS)

1. Early Flowering
e.g. 'Nelly Moser'
(Can be subdivided
into colour sections)
	Early Flowering
	1. Evergreen Group
	    e.g. *C. armandii*
	2. Alpina Group
	    e.g. *C. alpina* 'Frances Rivis'
	3. Macropetala Group
	    e.g. *C. macropetala* 'Markham's Pink'
	4. Montana Group
	    e.g. *C. montana* 'Mayleen'
	5. Rockery Group
	    e.g. *C. cartmanii* 'Joe'

2. Late Flowering
e.g. 'Jackmanii'
(Can be subdivided
into colour sections)
	Late Flowering
	6. Herbaceous Group
	    e.g. *C. integrifolia* 'Rosea'
	7. Viticella Group
	    e.g. *C. viticella* 'Mme Julia Correvon'
	8. Texensis Group
	    e.g. *C. texensis* 'Gravetye Beauty'
	9. Orientalis Group
	    e.g. *C. orientalis* 'Bill Mackenzie'
	10. Late Species Group
	    e.g. *C. flammula*

Roses

Hybridising of clematis and roses on a big scale started in the last century. Hybridising of clematis, because of the advent of wilt, ceased in the last century about 1880 and has only recommenced, on a small scale, in the last 30 years. Hybridising of roses, however, has continued on an increasing scale throughout the last 100 years and there is, therefore, a bewildering and immense number to choose from.

For the purposes of matching with clematis we can conveniently divide roses into three main groups - Climbing, Shrub and Bedding (Bush).

PLATE 19. Climbing
Roses round a window.

Climbing Group

The Climbing Group or Ascending Group (Climbing Old and Modern Roses) is
subdivided into two sub-groups - Climbing and Ramblers.

A. The Climbing Roses are stiff-stemmed, some have single blooms, are usually
scented, can repeat flower (remontant or recurrent) and need little pruning
(see Plate 19). New Climbers are not produced on the same scale as Bedding Roses.
Amongst the new Climbers are Climbing Hybrid Teas and Floribundas. A new
Climber may become popular every few years but many of the best come from the
last century or early this century, proving their worth with time. Examples of
Climbers would be 'Pink Perpétue', 'Compassion', 'Zephirine Drouhin'. We have
recently witnessed the advent of the Miniature Climbing Rose.

B. The Rambler Roses have fleshy stems, often have clusters of flowers, usually produce
one flush of blooms and frequently need severe pruning. They are less popular than the
Climbers because of lack of repeat flowering and a tendency of some to mildew.
Examples of true Ramblers would be 'American Pillar', 'Dorothy Perkins' and 'Excelsa'.

'New Dawn' (see Plate 20), 'Albéric Barbier', 'Emily Gray' and 'Albertine' have
some of the characteristics of the Climbing Group.

PLATE 20. The
Rambler 'New Dawn'
tumbling over a wall.
An excellent grower and
a perfect foil for most
clematis.

PLATE 21. The Modern Shrub Rose 'Chinatown' stands on its own in a shrubbery to give colour from large blooms for a long period.

Shrub Group

Shrub Roses are as old as time. Many definitions are offered but for our purposes we can regard a Shrub Rose as one that can stand alone as a specimen when required. They can, of course, be planted in groups for even greater impact and they have the great virtues of hardiness, beauty and fragrance although some only flower once. Examples would be 'Canary Bird', 'Cornelia', 'Frühlingsgold' and 'Penelope'. Some, such as the Bourbons, may flower again in the autumn. The Hybrid Musks are continuous blooming. Modern Shrub Roses have been developed that give a longer flowering period, for example, 'Ballerina', 'Chinatown' (see Plate 21) and 'Fred Loads'.

There is a small but interesting sub-group - the Spreading or Ground Cover section. Examples would be 'Nozomi' (see Plate 22) , 'Grouse' and 'Red Blanket'.

PLATE 22. The Ground Cover Rose 'Nozomi' is an excellent background for clematis.

PLATE 23. This bush of a Hybrid Tea shows the typical large blooms of such a rose.

Bedding Group

Bedding Roses are often employed for mass effect in beds devoted to them alone. They can also be used in groups in plant borders. They are colourful, hardy, and repeat flower. There are two sub-groups.

A. The Hybrid Teas (Large Flowered Bush) not only offer a choice of colours but most are scented. The blooms are often single and some can be of outstanding beauty of shape (see Plate 23). Examples would be 'Peace', 'Elina' and 'Fragrant Cloud'.

B. The Floribundas (Cluster Flowered Bush) have clusters of flowers, offer a great range of colour, an almost continuous flowering, and usually, but not always (e.g. 'Fragrant Delight'), lack fragrance. Examples of Floribundas would be 'Iceberg', 'Mountbatten', 'Queen Elizabeth' and 'Pink Parfait' (see Plate 24). (The shorter of the Floribundas are now termed Patio Roses - for small areas and front of borders, for example, 'Topsi', 'Anna Ford', 'Sweet Magic'.)

A developing sub-section is that of Miniature Roses - for edges, rockeries and pot culture. Examples are 'Baby Masquerade', 'Darling Flame', 'New Penny' and 'Starina'.

The major rose group for matching clematis is the Climbing Group, both being climbers. However, clematis can also climb on Shrubs and their clambering habit also allows them to be used with the Bedding Group.

PLATE 24. The beautiful Floribunda 'Pink Parfait' shows how clusters of blooms are typical of this group.

We can depict our grouping of roses in the following table:

Table II
THE THREE ROSE GROUPS

GROUP 1.	**Climbing** (Climbing Old and Modern Roses) A. **Climbers** e.g. 'Compassion' B. **Ramblers** e.g. 'American Pillar'
GROUP 2.	**Shrub** (Old and Modern) e.g. 'Canary Bird' (A sub-section is the Spreading Group, e.g. 'Nozomi')
GROUP 3.	**Bedding** A. **Hybrid Teas** (Large Flowered Bush), e.g. 'Peace' B. **Floribunda** (Cluster Flowered Bush), e.g. 'Queen Elizabeth' (There are sub-sections of Miniature Roses, e.g. 'Tom Thumb' and Patio Roses, e.g. 'Anna Ford')

PLATE 25. The ternate leaf (three leaflets) of a Large Flowered Clematis.

HABIT

Clematis

It is a surprise to many to know that the genus *Clematis* belongs to the family of plants Ranunculacae which is in common with plants such as buttercups and hellebores. It ceases to be a surprise when you know the range of the clematis and *C. marmoraria*, for instance, has flowers not dissimilar to those of a buttercup. Some of the blooms of the wild clematis can look like a hellebore.

The clematis is classed as a woody plant although we tend to get to know the plant in its early days when the stems are green and soft. After three to four years, however, the stems become woody, tough, and brown (see Figure 1). The plant is now much hardier, resists infections including wilt, and has a deserved reputation for toughness; so tough that some are said to be over a century old.

Most clematis plants climb and to do this use the stem (petiole) of a leaf for twisting round a support. One group of clematis do not have this facility and so they can only clamber and scramble. These are in the Herbaceous Group.

Most clematis lose their leaves in the winter, i.e. they are deciduous. This can give a barren appearance and with black leaves can be somewhat unsightly. There are remedies for this. Some climbers can be pruned in the autumn after flowering and this greatly reduces any unsightliness. Furthermore, clematis grown with other plants including roses are less conspicuous. A few clematis, mostly spring flowering, are evergreen.

The leaves of clematis vary from Large Flowered to Small Flowered. In the Large Flowered the leaves are usually ternate (three leaflets – see Plate 25) and are opposite (a pair of leaves are opposite one another at a node on a stem). This general pattern may vary slightly from plant to plant. In the Small Flowered there is much greater variation and there may be 5-7 leaflets; this helps to distinguish one group of Small Flowered clematis from another.

Clematis are self-clinging. The stem of the leaf, petiole, is used as a tendril and twists around a plant stem or artificial support (see Figure 2). The petiole gets thicker and stronger according to the weight it has to bear. Cleverly, the stem helps itself in another way. The stem coils to make a spring (see Figure 3). With the force

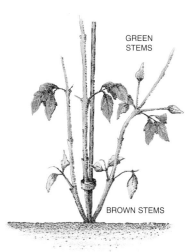

GREEN STEMS

BROWN STEMS

Figure 1. After 2-3 years lower green stems turn brown and become tougher as well as more resistant to wilt.

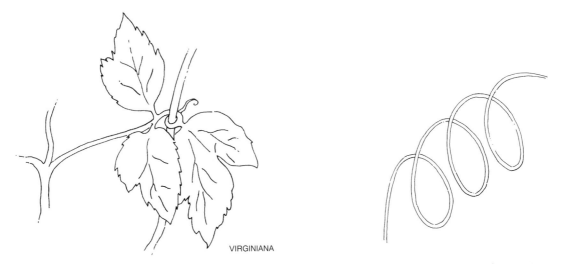

Figure 2. Coiling of petiole to grasp a support in *C.virginiana*. Figure 3. Coiling of petiole to make a spring.

of the wind there is a tug on the spring which gives and yet resists.

An extraordinary feature of clematis is the enormous variation in height. At one end, the shortest clematis is but 4 cm. (1½in.) in height. This is the delightful New Zealand clematis *C. marmoraria* (from the Marble Mountains – see Plate 13). So at one extreme we have rockery clematis. At the other extreme clematis that go soaring 12m. (40ft.) or more into a tree. These are the Montana clematis (see Plate 12). In between are the short herbaceous, Alpina, and Macropetala Groups, the medium height of the Large Flowered, Texensis, and Orientalis Groups and the taller Jackmanii, Viticella, Late Species and Evergreen Groups.

Clematis have one outstanding feature in the bloom. The petals are aborted. Instead the sepals take on the features of the petals. The botanists now give the name of tepals to these sepals. So instead of petals we have tepals - which look the same. Otherwise its structure is the same as the rose - it has stamens (male reproductive organ) and a pistil (female reproductive organ) made up of a number of carpels. It is pollinated by insects (see Figure 4).

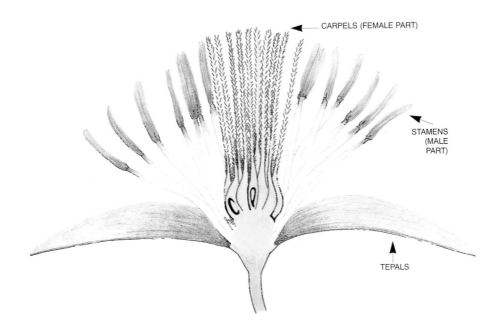

Figure 4. A section of 'Vitalba' showing the structure of a clematis.

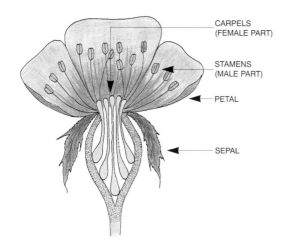

Figure 5. Structure of a rose.

CARPELS
(FEMALE PART)

STAMENS
(MALE PART)

PETAL

SEPAL

PLATE 26. The five leaflets of glossy rose leaves.

Roses

The rose belongs to the genus *Rosa* in the family Rosaceae. It grows in a variety of forms - Prostrate, Miniature Bush, Small Bush (sometimes termed a Patio Rose), Bush, Shrub, Standard and Climbing.

Although thorns can help, the climbing forms have no sure means of clinging to a support - thus they lean on the support and have to be tied to it to be secure. They can be made, with patience and time, to grow around a post or pillar.

The leaves alternate on the stem and the latter may have bracts. The leaves of roses have 5-7 leaflets which are usually glossy (see Plate 26). While normally a shade of green they can vary, especially Shrub Roses, producing attractive bronze, grey-green, crimson, etc.

The basic structure of the rose flower is like the clematis - it has petals, stamens (the male reproductive organ) and a pistil (the female reproductive organ – see Figure 5). It is pollinated by insects although, unlike clematis, it has green sepals outside the petals. The seeds are protected in a hip.

It can be seen that the clematis has no difficulty in being a companion to the rose as it can match it whatever its height and wherever it goes. It can clamber over the prostrate forms of bushes or shrubs and is able to cling with its petioles to the shrubs or climbing forms. Once the rose is secure on its support the clematis will look after itself on it, unless the gardener guides it in a particular direction for a special purpose. Only exceptionally is care required in case a very vigorous rose or clematis swamps the other. Particularly vigorous clematis are the Montanas, *C. armandii*, *C. cirrhosa*, *C. fargesii* and amongst the roses, *R. filipes* 'Kiftsgate', one plant of the latter having been recorded as growing to 140ft. (42.7m.) wide.

FLOWER COLOUR

Clematis

The colour of the clematis flower can vary greatly - from white to dark purple. Yellow clematis are rare in the Large Flowered Group while there tends to be a predominance in the Large Flowered varieties of the dark blue, purple and mauve clematis. Hybridists have worked hard over the last century to produce a greater range of colours and have been successful. In the Large Flowered Clematis we now have white, off-white, pale yellow, pink, red, light violet, blue, dark blue and purple. For matching the rose flowers there is now an adequate number in all colours - except for yellow. We only have four pale yellows - 'Moonlight', 'Wada's Primrose',

PLATE 27. Large Flowered Yellow Clematis are rare. An exception is the near yellow of 'Guernsey Cream'. This bloom of the Early Large Flowered Group shows an attractive tinge of green, common in early flowering clematis.

COLOUR PLATE 28. 'Maigold' is a good example of a common and popular yellow Climbing Rose. Like 'Guernsey Cream' it flowers early.

'Guernsey Cream' (see Plate 27) and 'Lemon Chiffon'; all four are worthy plants. But in the Small Flowered species, yellows come into their own; in the Orientalis Group there is a range of yellows in a number of differently shaped flowers.

Usually the colour of the clematis is at its strongest in the young flower. As it matures in the sun it tends to get lighter. Hence the difficulty of describing the colour of a particular flower as it depends when you do it. The sunnier the climate the stronger the colour of the bloom. An interesting feature is that white flowers can develop a green tinge if grown in shade. This tends to occur in the spring or in the autumn. Far from being unsightly it can add attraction to the bloom. Clematis blooms are often more dramatic because of the conspicuous nature of the stamens. Especially is this so when a strong colour in the stamens are set against white tepals, for example 'Miss Bateman' or 'C. florida 'Bicolor', both of which make a strong impact though the former is much easier to grow than the latter. In matching with a rose bloom, the colour of the stamens and the tepals need to be taken into account.

Most clematis have a single colour. Occasionally there are two or more shades of a colour in the same flower, for example, 'Vyvyan Pennell'. A number are striped, i.e. there is a band of a different colour on a tepal, an example being 'Nelly Moser'.

The colour of clematis leaves can vary – green, dark green, grey-green, bright green. *C. cirrhosa* in winter can have leaves that appear dark red from below and *C. armandii* can have young leaves of bright purple.

Roses

In contrast to clematis, roses are never blue or near blue and while this is acceptable in many flowers, there is almost a revulsion to having this colour in roses. Otherwise, there is a wide choice of colours from white to pink to red to yellow to orange and many bicolours.

Many roses have a single colour but there is also more variety than in clematis. A bicolour is produced by the curving of a petal which leads to the inside and the outside of the petal being exposed. On some trusses of roses multicolours can be seen due to the fading of the blooms at a different rate. Some roses have striped flowers. As with clematis, rose petals change colour with exposure to the sun and with ageing.

The basic colours of rose leaves are light green, medium green, dark green and

PLATE 29. Multi-tepaled clematis are uncommon. Newly introduced 'Arctic Queen' is a fine example of this type and belongs to the Early Large Flowered Group.

bronze. In wild roses, however, unusual colours can add greatly to the charm of the flower - red, crimson, grey-green and these often vary with the time of the season.

In matching clematis and roses account must be taken of the colour of the leaves in the roses. In rose shrubs, when the flowers are gone, it is entirely a case of matching the clematis flower to the rose leaves.

Clematis are a natural colour foil to roses. The abundance of blue clematis flowers is a contrast to the many yellow and orange roses (see Plate 28) and, as many colours are in common to both plants, there is also room for harmonious matching.

FLOWER SHAPE

Clematis

A clematis bloom can be single, double – 'Sylvia Denny', or a multiple (up to 70 tepals) – 'Duchess of Edinburgh', 'Proteus' and 'Vyvyan Pennell'. One, 'Louise Rowe', can exhibit all three forms at the same time of flowering. Those with

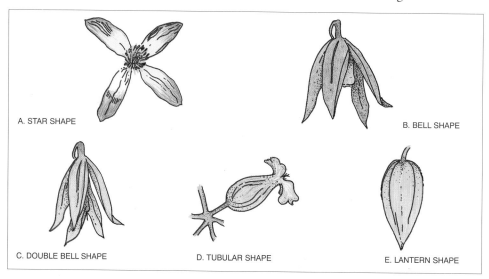

Figure 6. The shapes of clematis blooms.

A. STAR SHAPE

B. BELL SHAPE

C. DOUBLE BELL SHAPE

D. TUBULAR SHAPE

E. LANTERN SHAPE

PLATE 30. Among the uncommon single Climbing Roses is found one of the most beautiful of all – 'Mermaid'. Slow to start it ultimately produces a large plant of incomparable blossoms and fine foliage.

multiple tepals look like a peony (see Plate 29), reminding one that the clematis and the peony were once members of the same family; the peony has now made a family of its own, Paeonaceae. In the autumn, doubles and the multiples usually produce single blooms as a bonus.

Many clematis will open to a flat, or saucer-like, bloom but there are many variations on this. There is a tiny blue-white star in *C. flammula*, a single bell in *C. alpina*, a double bell in *C. macropetala*, a tubular bloom in *C. texensis* and lantern-shaped blooms in *C. tangutica*.

Roses

Roses can be single such as 'Mermaid' (see Plate 30), double like 'Masquerade' or multipetalled as in 'Peace' while Hybrid Teas tend to be the lovely high-centred shape. There is much variation in Old Roses - quartered, open-cupped, globular, rosette-shaped, pompon and some of these intriguing shapes are to be seen in the New English Roses.

Figure 7. Some of the shapes of rose blooms.

PLATE 31. Clematis 'Lawsoniana' from the 19th century has a bloom of up to 10in. (25cm.), the size of a dinner plate! The plant is tall growing and ideal for extending round a corner or growing into a tall Climbing Rose. It belongs to the Early Large Flowered Group.

FLOWER SIZE

Clematis

The largest blooms are in clematis flowering in spring and summer while the Jackmanii Group of late summer are almost as large. They can extend to 25cm. (10in.) - the size of a dinner plate (see Plate 31). 'W.E.Gladstone' is said to have the largest bloom. The blooms of the Viticella Group are of medium size but produce colour by a mass of bloom. In general the smaller the size of flower the greater the number of flowers. The small flowers of *C. montana* are produced in their thousands. The smallest blooms of all, as in *C. flammula*, produce myriads making a plant three metres (10ft.) high covered in bloom and with an astonishing fragrance.

The number of blooms is again variable - in general the larger the bloom the smaller the number produced. A well-established large-flowered variety can produce 500 blooms while in the Jackmanii Group this can go up to 1,500 blooms and in the Viticella/Montana Groups even more. In some of the species the number is beyond counting. The Japanese, who specialise in growing clematis in pots, can expect to produce up to 200 blooms in a pot plant.

Roses

In roses the larger blooms are to be found in the Hybrid Teas and those that have taken on a climbing habit, i.e. the Climbing Hybrid Teas (see Plate 32). The production of large blooms can be encouraged by severe pruning, disbudding and generous feeding – well-known to the exhibitors who produce outstandingly large blooms or specimen blooms at rose shows such as 'Peace', 'Admiral Rodney', 'Alec's Red', 'Grandpa Dickson', 'Red Devil'. Size is not enough as marks will also be given for perfection of shape, colour and fragrance. Light pruning results in more, but smaller, blooms.

In the Floribundas and Ramblers the emphasis is on quantity of colourful blooms and the size of individual examples is sacrificed to this.

PLATE 32. 'Compassion' is one of the Climbing Roses with a large bloom. It has been said that if there is only room for one Climbing Rose in a garden then the choice falls on 'Compassion' for the beauty, size and scent of its blooms, its vigour, its reliability and its continuous flowering.

Shrub Roses can produce large blooms but more commonly the picture is one of a large number of small, beautiful blooms.

Smaller flowers are to be found, of course, in the Miniature Roses but there is no lack of lovely shapes.

FRAGRANCE

Clematis

It would be pleasant to say that the Large Flowered Clematis are heavy with fragrance. This is not so, with perhaps the exception of 'Fair Rosamond' (see Plate 33). With the 'eye of faith' scent can be experienced in 'Ascotiensis', 'Barbara Jackman', 'Duchess of Edinburgh', 'Marie Boisselot' and 'Sylvia Denny'. That does

PLATE 33. 'Fair Rosamond' is the only Large Flowered Clematis to claim a fair degree of fragrance. Being early in flower it wears a tinge of green.

37

PLATE 34. 'Zephirine Drouhin' would be on everyone's list for delicious fragrance. A popular rose since the last century with the unusual merit of being thornless.

not mean that you cannot have scent in clematis. Indeed, you can have heavy fragrance for most of the year. The first clematis in the spring, *C. cirrhosa* has scent and is followed by *C. armandii*, overpowering in its scent; in March the fragrance of the beautiful clusters of these pearly white flowers has to be experienced to be believed. The flowering year ends with another outpouring of fragrance – in *C. flammula*, *C. triternata* 'Rubro-marginata' and *C. terniflora*. In between there is fragrance in the Montana, the Herbaceous and the Orientalis Groups.

Roses

In the rose world we look to the Old Shrub Roses for abundance of scent and words cannot describe the diversity, subtlety, and intensity of their fragrance. The sweet briar 'Lady Penzance, even has fragrant foliage!

Fragrance is to be found in many of the Hybrid Teas such as 'Fragrant Cloud', 'Lady Sylvia', 'My Choice', 'Ophelia', and 'Prima Ballerina'.

Fragrance takes second place to colour in the Floribundas but a few are very fragrant, for example, 'English Miss', 'Fragrant Delight', 'Margaret Merril', 'Scented Air', 'Sheila's Perfume' and 'Arthur Bell'.

There is more scent in the Climbers than in the Ramblers. Fragrant popular Climbers include 'Compassion', 'Climbing Crimson Glory', 'Gloire de Dijon', 'Golden Showers', 'Madame Grégoire Staechelin', 'Maigold', 'Meg', 'Mermaid', 'Schoolgirl', and 'Zephirine Drouhin' (see Plate 34).

Fragrance can be found in a few of the less typical Ramblers – especially 'Albertine', 'Albéric Barbier', 'New Dawn', and 'Kiftsgate'. There is a strong subjective factor in the choice of the most fragrant bouquet in a rose but 'Zephirine Drouhin', 'Albertine', 'Fragrant Cloud', 'Gloire de Dijon', would be amongst the contenders for most rosarians.

We tend to match roses and clematis for colour why not for fragrance?

PLATE 35. Some of the Early Large Flowered Clematis produce fine seed heads. Here is a head from 'General Sikorski'.

SEEDS

Clematis

Clematis is one of the plants that can produce an effect with its seed heads alone. Everyone in Europe knows of 'Old Man's Beard'; the effect of a long beard produced by the sweeps of grey-white seed heads produced on the species *C. vitalba*, native to Europe. Native clematis of other countries produce the same effect. Especially fine heads are produced by the Alpina, Macropetala, Orientalis and the Late Species Groups. They can enhance the rose right through the winter. Indeed, they look their most dramatic frosted on a cold morning. The seeds make a cluster with a long feathery grey-white tail to each and these break off in the spring to float away in search of hospitable soil (see Plate 35).

In most clematis there are both male and female parts in the same flower. The pollen comes from the stamen and is deposited on the carpels in the centre of the flower. In a few clematis, and in particular the New Zealand clematis, some plants bear only male parts while others bear only female parts. In this group it is thus necessary to have both male and female plants in order to hybridise.

Rose

The rose is more careful of its offspring than the clematis. It offers protection to the seeds by wrapping them in a hip which comes in many choices of colours, from black to red, and in many shapes. Autumn and winter are enlivened by the display of hips as they are conspicuous in the shrub roses and can be as important a feature as the blooms. Indeed, some are grown for their hips rather than their blossoms. The hips attract animals and birds and through them the seed finds a fertile medium for growth.

Careful planning could produce the combination of the seed heads of the Early Flowering Clematis with rose blooms; or Late Flowering Roses with the seed heads of the Orientalis clematis; or the matching of ripe hips with a suitable foil of clematis; or bright hips against the grey-white background of clematis seed heads (see Plate 36).

Like most clematis the rose bears male and female parts on the same flower.

For seeds to be produced in a clematis or rose the pollen from the male part of that plant or another plant has to be conveyed to the stigma of the female part of

PLATE 36. Nature has contrived to bring together the seed heads of wild clematis 'Vitalba' and the hips of a wild rose.

the plant. From there the pollen makes a tube down the style to the ovary where its nucleus combines with the nucleus therein. Man can interfere in this process by introducing a pollen of his choice to the stigma of his choice and thus in a directed fashion produce a new combination which will become a unique new flower, hopefully with the virtues that will appeal to the gardener.

The pollen is conveyed from anther to pistil by the activity of insects and the force of the wind. As yet it is not possible to cross clematis with rose as they belong to different families.

HARDINESS

Clematis

Some clematis – the Alpina and Macropetala Groups – can survive in temperatures down to -40°. Clematis are grown in very cold countries such as Russia and Canada and here special precautions are taken. The clematis are cut down to the ground in the autumn and the crown of the plants are protected with straw, etc. A thaw is more damaging than a deep persistent frost, however, therefore the aim is to insulate the soil and so maintain the low temperature. In very cold countries there is a tendency to grow short Large Flowered Clematis so that less growth is necessary for the brief growing period. Large Flowered clematis which have a good reputation in a cold climate are 'Victoria' (see Plate 37), 'Hagley Hybrid', 'Comtesse de Bouchaud', 'Gipsy Queen' and 'Perle d'Azur'. In extremely cold climates the Large Flowered Clematis can be grown in containers and brought into shelter for the winter.

Wind can damage the clematis by tearing the fragile petioles away from their support. The damage can also allow the wilt fungus into the plant through the damaged areas. A cold wind can kill a clematis when it would otherwise survive the cold. Clematis profit from the shelter of the rose.

Roses

Roses are among the most hardy of garden plants – especially Shrub Roses – and can be grown in countries with low temperatures in winter. In severe conditions the crown of the rose can be protected by a layer of fern, straw, or other material - even newspaper. In exceptional conditions the whole bush can be wrapped in a protective

layer. Snow is a fine insulator. As with clematis, damage can be done by a rapid thaw followed by refreezing.

Protection from a cold wind helps survival as it does with the clematis. In windy sites the rose can be helped by a partial pruning in the autumn to reduce wind resistance; loosening the roots can lead to the death of a plant.

ROOTS

Clematis

The roots of clematis are of two kinds. In the Large Flowered the roots are pivotal, thong-like, or bootlace-like (see Plate 38). They can go down 1 metre (3ft.) into the soil. In the Small Flowered Clematis the roots are quite different, they are thread-like or fibrous (see Plate 39). The bootlaces will stand a gentle spreading out; the fibrous roots should not be touched.

PLATE 38. The lace-like roots so common in the Large Flowered Groups and the Viticella Group.

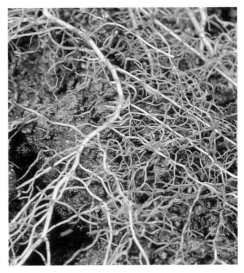

PLATE 39. The fibrous roots so common in the Small Flowered Groups. They need a gentle management at planting.

PLATE 40. The strong roots of a Bedding (Bush) Rose. The roots belong to the stock wild rose on which the Bedding Rose has been grafted.

Roses

Roses are not usually grown on their own roots, unless they are grown from cuttings. Roses are budded on to the stock of wild roses (see Plate 40). At one time this applied to clematis but it has been abandoned as clematis grow very well from cuttings; sometimes grafting is still employed to produce a supply quickly of a new clematis. A rose bush can be a considerable obstruction to wind and thus the rose needs strong splayed out roots to anchor it to the ground. In exposed positions it is helpful to reduce the amount of foliage by partial pruning in the autumn.

FAULTS

Clematis

These are few. Some gardeners complain that clematis can display rather a lot of brown or black stem in their lower parts. This is much less noticeable if grown with other plants such as roses or hidden by a Shrub Rose. Again, the top half of the clematis can be bent down to cover the lower bare parts. Furthermore, judicious pruning can cause the plant to break from near ground level. Another trick is to grow a short clematis with a particularly tall clematis so that the shorter can cover the bare portions of the taller.

Another complaint is that the brown stalks of clematis can look unsightly on the rose in winter. There is a solution. The clematis such as the Jackmanii and Viticella Groups can be pruned back to about three feet in the autumn. The stems are brought together with a tie making the clematis almost invisible. Why not prune to the ground? The three feet or so of stem can protect the crown in a frosty winter and the pruning can then be finished in spring.

Another complaint is that clematis, if left unpruned, make a conspicuous tangle. This is the result of defective pruning. Once a tangle is produced, prune, even in the autumn, just below the tangle and all will be tidy. Never prune into the thick brown stems of the Large Flowered Clematis. They may give up the ghost!

Roses

Roses have few faults as can be judged by their popularity although some regret the loss of fragrance in the modern hybrid varieties. This is rapidly being corrected.

Some expect only to be able to grow roses in a clay soil but roses grow well in any well-nourished soil. Others deplore the rather rigid, regimented planting of the rose, making blobs of stark, startling colour. Contemporary fashion is accepting this criticism and moving towards planting roses with other plants. An obvious companion is the clematis - and hence this book.

MYTHS

Clematis

There are but two. One states that a clematis likes its feet in the shade and its head in the sun. It is not the shade that the roots require, it is the water that lies in the shade. If clematis are given adequate watering and adequate mulching they will flower in full sun.[2] A second myth states that clematis enjoy an alkaline soil which comes from the observation that they flourish in chalk soil. It is not the alkalinity, however, that encourages the clematis, rather it is that chalk holds deposits of water and this is what the plant is after. Given water it will flourish in any soil as long as there are no extremes of acidity or alkalinity.

Roses

There are few myths in the case of the rose. Its existence in such wealth of numbers over a long period of time has brought familiarity which in turn has exploded most of the myths.

It has been said that modern roses are never scented but acquaintance with them shows this not to be true. Another myth relates to pruning which is held to be difficult. In fact it is one of the easiest flowers to prune.

FLOWERING TIMES

Clematis Through the Year

As can be seen from the following table, a garden can have clematis in bloom throughout the year. This is a surprise as the eye-catching Large Flowered Clematis are so conspicuous in mid season that other groups tend to be forgotten.

Early Spring	*Clematis armandii*
Mid Spring	*Clematis alpina*
	Clematis macropetala
Late Spring	*Clematis montana*; Early Large Flowered Clematis
Early Summer	*Clematis chrysocoma*; mid term Large Flowered Clematis
Midsummer	Late Large Flowered hybrids, Herbaceous Clematis
Late Summer	*Viticella* hybrids, Herbaceous Clematis
Early Autumn	*Texensis* hybrids
Mid Autumn	*Clematis tangutica*; Very Late Large Flowered Clematis
Late Autumn	*Clematis terniflora*
Early Winter	*Clematis napulensis* (for the conservatory in most areas)
Mid/Late Winter	*Clematis cirrhosa*

2. Howells, J. *Growing Clematis.* 1993. Cassell. London.

PLATE 41. The sweetly scented, very popular, 'Albertine' exhausts itself with a glorious display early in the rose season and few blooms appear later. Its foliage after flowering makes an excellent support for clematis.

PLATE 42. Deservedly popular rose 'Pink Perpétue' tries a continuous display through the rose season. Its slightly purple fluorescence perfectly matches the purple clematis.

Roses Through the Year

In general roses can be found in bloom in the garden from late spring into late autumn - this latter depending on the severity and onset of winter frosts. The peak period is early and midsummer.

Some roses, especially Shrub and Rambler Roses, may flower once only for a period of a few weeks. Some flower early depending on the climatic conditions in late spring and early summer with examples such as the Shrubs 'Canary Bird' and *Rosa* 'Hugonis' and the Climbers 'Meg', 'Maigold', and 'Madame Grégoire Staechelin'. Most will flower once in early and midsummer and include examples 'Albertine' (see Plate 41), 'Albéric Barbier', 'American Pillar'. The crop of a few

PLATE 43. 'Galway Bay' manages at least two crops of flowers and the latest can be in the autumn. Its glowing colours perfectly match the many purple clematis.

may come late with examples such as the Climbers 'Dorothy Perkins' and 'Crimson Shower' and the Shrub 'Frühlingsmorgen'.

Some roses will repeat flower producing two main crops of flowers and examples would be the Climbers 'Casino', 'Dublin Bay', 'Galway Bay' (see Plate 43), 'Golden Showers' and 'Zephirine Drouhin' (see Plate 34).

Some not only have two crops a season but also have substantial crops in between which gives the impression of being continuous or perpetually flowering. Examples of these would be many Hybrid Tea and Floribunda Roses, some of the English Roses, hence their popularity, and Climbing Roses such as 'Compassion', 'Pink Perpétue' (see Plate 42), 'Mermaid', 'New Dawn' and 'Gloire de Dijon' (rather sparsely).

Matching Flowering Times of Roses and Clematis

Consideration of the flowering periods of clematis and roses helps to determine our strategy in the planting of the two companions. The colour of 'Lady Betty Balfour' would blend well with the colour of the rose 'Maigold' but one, the rose, flowers in late spring and the other, the clematis, in late summer. So matching here would not be possible. We need to be familiar with the flowering times of all rose and clematis groups.

As many clematis flower before any roses, the latter can be used as support for the former while benefiting themselves by having early colour given to the rose plants.

The peak flowering of roses and clematis coincides and offers an opportunity to match the colour of the companions. Very late flowering roses can be involved in this right into the autumn.

As the clematis flower later than the roses, the plants of the latter can act as support for late flowering clematis and themselves gain from late colour on the rose plants.

In general the habits of roses are more predictable while clematis are particularly responsive to the climatic conditions - a very hot summer can make for a short season of flowering while a dull wet summer can prolong the flowering period. This can also apply to roses but usually to a lesser extent.

CHAPTER TWO
Organising the Good Companions

GENERAL PRINCIPLES

Our discussion of the rose and clematis has revealed great potential for matching them together and both are now popular garden plants. The rose has been so for a long time while the clematis is enjoying a comeback. Formal ways of presenting the rose are giving way to less formal and the moment is right to combine the rose and clematis.

In the main the clematis is either a climber or clamberer and a few are herbaceous. The rose, however, has definite groups with well-marked qualities – climbers, shrubs, bedders. The clematis is predominantly a climber therefore its ideal companion is the Climbing Rose. It can also make use of the support of a Shrub Rose and, in certain circumstances, clamber over a Bedding Rose. Consequently, prime attention must be given to the Climbing Rose and the clematis as companions.

In general the habits of the rose and clematis are similar and it is rare that one plant is too vigorous for the other.

For a perfect combination two areas need special attention:

1. The use of rose and clematis for colour matching in the garden.
2. Utilising the flowering time of both to maximum advantage.

Both topics now require further discussion.

COLOUR MATCHING

A general notion of some of the principles of colour appreciation will help us in our desire to match clematis and roses. At the same time it must be said that many gardeners have an inborn capacity for matching colours and can trust their own judgement.

The colour wheel
The break up of light can be seen in the rainbow. It can also be seen in the colour wheel which is simply a representation of colours of the rainbow in a full circle. The sequence of colour is red, yellow, orange, green, blue, violet and all are classed as 'hues'. There are three primary colours - red, yellow and blue – so-called because by mixing them, all colours can be produced. Midway between the three primary colours are three secondary or intermediary colours - orange, green, violet and these are produced by mixing two primary colours, for example, red and yellow making orange.

The colours on the wheel merge into one another, e.g. red merges into orange on one side and into violet on the other.

The colours opposite one another are contrasting colours (in technical language 'complementary' – see Plate 46):

Red	to	Green
Yellow	to	Violet
Blue	to	Orange

Complementary colours, such as blue and orange, when added together make white or grey.

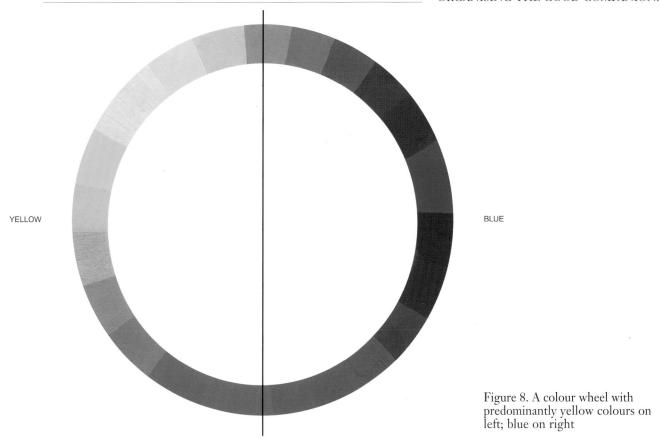

YELLOW

BLUE

Figure 8. A colour wheel with predominantly yellow colours on left; blue on right

Colours close to one another in colouring are in harmony (see Plate 45):

Orange	and	Yellow
Red	and	Orange
Red	and	Pink
White	and	Pink
Greeny-yellow	and	Reddish-violet

Mixing a hue with white produces a 'tint', e.g. red and white make pink. Mixing a hue with grey or black produces a 'shade', e.g. grey-green.

It is possible to divide the spectrum of colour into two parts by running a line through green and red. On one side blue is the predominant colour and in the other half yellow is predominant. Matching on one side of the line results in harmonious colours such as salmon-pink, red and maroon, blues, lilacs and purple. In a general way matching the two sides of the spectrum can give good contrast results, for example, red and green.

Changes in colour

Colour appreciation can be influenced by:

1. The brightness of the colour.
2. The area of the colour.
3. Saturation of the colour.
4. Nearness of colours to one another.
5. Our emotions.
6. Light.

1. We have to take account of the brightness or intensity of a colour.
   Yellow is a very bright colour. Orange and red are bright.

PLATE 44. A small amount of yellow, rose 'Casino' here, is sufficient to match a much larger area of blue, here clematis 'Lasurstern'.

Green and blue are less bright. Violet is very dark.

To match the brightness of yellow calls for four times the amount of violet (see Plate 44). (This is a matter of importance in matching the many yellow roses and the many violet clematis.)

To match the brightness of orange calls for three times the amount of violet.

Red and green are equal in brightness. Thus they will match in equal amounts of colour.

2. The impact of a particular colour will be influenced by its areas.

Because blue is so common in clematis it will often be available for matching. Because yellow and orange are frequent in roses, they will often be available for matching. However, they must not be matched in equal amounts as yellow and orange are brighter than violet. For the best effect a violet clematis three times the size of an orange clematis or a violet clematis four times the size of a yellow clematis should be used.

Red and green are of equal brightness and so red clematis can be used in equal amounts on green rose leaves.

Orange roses and blue clematis could be used in equal amounts but blue clematis always have a tinge of violet and allowance must be made for this.

3. We also need to take purity (saturation) of the colour into account.

A light tone of a light colour should be planted with a dark tone of a darker colour, for example, light yellow on a deep purple – a very useful combination with yellow roses and violet clematis. This is termed tonal order. Another example would be a pink on a deep violet. The reverse should never be used, for example, a dark yellow with a light violet.

4. The impact of a colour can also be influenced by the colours near to it.
For example, yellow and violet together both look brighter than when apart. Thus these colours are good combinations for clematis and roses. Red and green are also bright colours and enhance one another.

5. Our emotions are also involved and respond to colour.
Colours that harmonize produce a reaction of tranquillity. Colours that are in contrast produce a reaction of excitement. Red, orange, yellow, are vibrant, exciting, aggressive, warm. Blues and violets are cool, sombre, passive and soothing.

6. The quality of light affects the garden.
Light intensity increases from winter to summer. The time of day affects light. In the morning, for example, there is an element of pale yellow in the light, while at noon there is white light. In the afternoon there is rich gold in the light and magenta in the evening. Red is conspicuous at midday and blue and violet at twilight.
Light from the north is the coolest. It has a minimum of red, orange and yellow and is the best light for colour matching.
Light backgrounds with bright colours look larger or more distant but dark backgrounds with subdued colours look smaller and closer.

Application of colour theory
Taking account of theory helps to enhance natural flair and personal tastes. Here we need to consider:

1. The colours available in roses and clematis.
2. That green is ever present.
3. The importance of blues and yellows in our project.
4. The significance of other colours.
5. Some suggested matchings.

1. Available Colours in this Field
We need to note colours available to us in roses and clematis.

Roses	**Clematis**
White	White
Pink	Pink
Red	Red
Yellow	Very few yellows
Orange	No orange
No blues or mauves	Many blues and mauves
No blacks	No blacks
Green in leaves	Green in leaves

2. Green
It is easy to overlook the obvious, as far as colour in the garden is concerned, and we need to remind ourselves that the predominant colour is green. Indeed, most flowers

PLATE 45. The colours of rose 'Iceberg' and clematis 'Margot Koster' complement one another.

PLATE 46. The colours of rose 'Handel' forming a pleasing contrast to clematis 'Victoria'.

have matching green leaves. Thus green is a background to most flowers. In matching two flowers in the garden we are, to some extent, matching green with green, i.e. a flower with green leaves with another flower with green leaves. Of course, there are some flowers and plants that have leaves which are not green and are of other colours - silver, grey, bronze, yellow, red, shades of green and variegated.

Being next to green changes a colour. For example, yellow against green looks more orange than it really is as the yellow makes the green look more blue. Green in general is a pleasing colour and the absence of it makes us think of arid areas such as deserts. It is possible to have a garden with matching green plants alone and very effective it can be.

It is remarkable how excellently nature matches roses or clematis to green leaves - usually producing harmony. We immediately become aware of this harmony if the leaves die producing either a brown or a black background to our plants. We have an immediate desire to cut away the disfiguring brown or black background.

In matching rose and clematis we should, of course, attempt to match the colour of the two flowers if they are flowering together. Even if we cannot do this and can only match the flower to the greenery of the other, much will still have been accomplished.

3. Blues and Yellows
No blue clematis is truly blue. Indeed, it is rare to have pure blue flowers in nature. Checking with a colour chart shows that there is always an element of purple in the so-called 'blue' clematis. In the purple there is red which emerges in photographs of clematis taken in the sun. While clematis 'Perle d'Azur' and 'Prince Charles' can look like light blue clematis from a distance they are in fact light violet.

On a spectrum of strong to weak the shades amongst the blues of clematis are as follows: purple - violet - mauve - lavender

The blues of clematis offer contrast to the many shades of yellow and orange found in roses - in the right proportions, as was discussed earlier (see page 48). The proportion of violet to yellow should be 4 : 1. Too much yellow swamps the clematis which will not be noticed. A small amount of yellow will light up the violet clematis.

As there are so many blue/violet clematis we have a unique opportunity to produce one of the most vivid combinations in the garden – orange/yellow roses with blue/violet clematis.

4. Other Colours

White is a good background for most colours except cream and grey; with too much violet it produces a sombre scene. Accordingly, red, deep pink, light violet clematis are more striking with white roses but a subdued combination of white roses and mauve clematis can still be beautiful and relieve a part of the garden which has too much colour. Rose 'New Dawn', blush in colour, is a rose of outstanding merit as a light background for clematis.

Small splashes of white, yellow, orange and red will light up the scene in the garden but they should be used sparingly.

The many shades of violet clematis will blend but offer no excitement and need contrasting colours such as yellow, orange or white to bring them to life.

Red can be a difficult colour as it can be too bright and eye-catching. Like the other bright colours it needs to be used in moderation (see Plate 47). Brickwork is a difficult colour with red or pink blooms.

Pink is easier to handle than red, which applies to all tints and is why the unadventurous, for safety, use only pastel colours in the garden.

Grey and silver are useful as background colour both for the bright and sombre colours; the many violet clematis respond to grey and silver leaves when found on a rose.

For dark corners use white, pink, salmon, yellow and light blue colours. Some clematis, such as 'Twilight' and 'Dr Ruppel', have a touch of fluorescence, as does the rose 'Pink Perpétue', which lightens dark corners.

Yellow can be cooled by cream, white, or blue. Blue adds clarity to white flowers.

Green, often the background colour in a rose bush, especially when out of flower, can be brightened by white, yellow, pink and red clematis (see Plate 48). Violet is not in disharmony but the effect is more subdued.

Too many contrasts in the garden produce a feeling of restlessness.

5. Matchings

Some harmonious matchings are as follows:

Pink roses	and	Violet clematis
Red roses	and	Mauve clematis
Light yellow roses	and	Pink clematis
Cream roses	and	Lilac clematis
White roses	and	Lilac clematis
Pink roses	and	Deep pink clematis
Deep pink roses	and	Pink clematis

| Deep pink roses | and | White clematis |
| Red roses | and | Pink clematis |

Contrasting colours are:

White roses	and	Red clematis
Yellow roses	and	Mauve clematis
Orange roses	and	Blue clematis
Red roses	and	Green leaves
Red roses	and	White clematis
Pink roses	and	Purple clematis

THE FLOWERING PERIODS

We know that in general clematis have a longer flowering period than the roses. This statement needs qualification; some roses flower early or in mid season and produce no further blooms. Some, however, produce another blush of bloom and a few can be in flower into the winter. Thus clematis can, in some circumstances, be used on roses before and after the roses flower. They can also bloom together as roses and clematis have the same peak period - in midsummer.

Two of the very early flowering clematis would not be suitable in combination due to their vigour - the Evergreen and Montana Groups. Three early flowering clematis groups, however, are suitable by their habit and time of flowering in early spring. These are the Alpinas, the Macropetalas and the Early Large Flowering Clematis.

Shrub and Climbing Roses offer the support that clematis need. This dictates the first method of combining roses and clematis – before the rose flowers.

In early and midsummer both roses and clematis are at their flowering peak. Here is the opportunity for colour matching of the blooms at its best. This dictates the second method of combination of rose and clematis - as the rose flowers.

As the flowering of roses wanes so the flowering of clematis continues - Jackmanii, Viticella, Texensis, Orientalis Groups and Late Species. The roses that have ceased flowering are available as support and as a background. This situation dictates the third method of combining rose and clematis - after the rose has flowered.

During the summer other groups of clematis can add colour to the rose – the Texensis and Herbaceous Groups – by close proximity below the rose. This dictates the fourth method of combination - the clematis at the foot of the rose.

While some clematis would embarrass the rose with their excess vigour, they can still be planted in areas nearby either to give colour to that corner of the garden before or after the rose blooms or to combine with the rose when it flowers. This dictates the fifth method of combination of rose and clematis - the clematis near the rose.

Our five methods of utilising clematis with roses are:

1. Before the rose flowers.
2. With the rose flowering.
3. After the rose flowers.
4. Under the rose.
5. Near the rose.

PLATE 47. Red is an eye-catching colour but can be too dominant in a garden unless used in moderation.

PLATE 48. The colours of rose 'Compassion' harmonise with those of clematis 'Ernest Markham' which contrasts with the green leaves of the rose.

PLATE 49. Two colours of clematis can be mixed together, as we see here, with 'Proteus' the lighter and 'Victoria' the darker colour. Even sombre colours, in harmony, can make a beautiful blend.

USING CLEMATIS

Experience in growing clematis has established that up to three clematis can be planted with each Climbing Rose.

A clematis is planted 1½-2ft. (45-62cm.) on either side of the rose; this makes two clematis. Another, at the same time, or later, can be planted alongside the rose; this makes three clematis for each rose.

The clematis can be selected to all flower together or can flower in sequence over a period of time. If the clematis flower together there is a maximum impact for a short period, an example being 'Perle d'Azur' on the rose 'Mermaid'. If they flower in sequence there is some colour for a long period. For example, a sequence could be an early season clematis such as 'Lasurstern'; a mid season clematis such as 'Hagley Hybrid', and a late season clematis such as 'Lady Betty Balfour'.

PLATE 50. Here we have the cheerful mingling of three colours – the blue 'General Sikorski', pink 'Hagley Hybrid' and red 'Madame Julia Correvon'.

If the clematis are planted to flower in sequence then all three clematis on a rose can be from the Large Flowered Group. It is also possible to have a clematis from three different groups, for example, a Macropetala for early flowering, a Large Flowered Clematis for mid season, and a Viticella for late season.

If all the clematis are planned to flower on the rose then they can be different varieties or all of one variety. The latter can give a dramatic effect over a short period, for example, a number of clematis 'General Sikorski' on the rose 'New Dawn'. If different varieties are selected they can be of similar or different colours (see Plate 49).

The three clematis on a Climbing Rose can be kept apart so that a particular type and colour is seen from a particular direction. Even more effective is to allow the three clematis to mingle and thus produce, with the rose, a great centre of interest (see Plate 50).

The two roses on either side of the rose can also extend outwards on a rope between two roses - festooning. On a pergola the clematis can reach the woodwork on either side of the Climbing Rose. Clematis can be guided to the rope or cross-piece with a cane, wire or string.

RELAXED GARDENING

Rosarians and clematarians will want to read on and any amount of detail will be acceptable to them. For some gardeners, however, combining the roses and clematis is a desirable event but one of many events in the garden. Thus a simple, general plan may be all that is required for them. Here is a simple plan.

Most matching takes place mid season. It must be borne in mind that it is sometimes difficult to get the timing right and, consequently, there is value in using flowers that are blooming continuously. There are roses and clematis that do this.

Choose a few easy roses given to continuous blooming such as 'New Dawn', 'Mermaid' and 'Pink Perpétue'. Choose also clematis given to long flowering, for example, 'Mrs Cholmondeley', 'Comtesse de Bouchaud', 'Margot Koster' (see lists which follow). It may be desirable first of all to focus on the rose and choose its most suitable companion.

As an insurance one can use three clematis of different flowering periods on a particular rose to make sure that one will be in flower when required so that a desirable matching takes place.

Remember many roses are yellow or orange and many clematis are mauve-blue.

This group of gardeners will require a comprehensive list of dependable clematis. Twelve are found below made up of the recommendations of the British Clematis Society combined with my own experience.

List of Popular Clematis

Name	Colour	Flowering	
'Miss Bateman'	White	Early season	(Plate 7)
'Marie Boisselot'	White	Mid season	(Plate 56)
'Huldine'	White	Late season	(Plate 68)
'Hagley Hybrid'	Pink	Mid season	(Plates 45, 50)
'Margot Koster'	Pink	Mid & late season	(Plate 71)
'Mme Julia Correvon'	Red	Mid season	(Plates 50, 70)
'Niobe'	Red	Mid season	(Plate 64)

'Lasurstern'	Deep Blue	Early season	(Plates 53, 63)
'Perle d'Azur'	Light violet	Mid season	(Plates 4, 44)
'Victoria'	Light blue-purple	Late season	(Plates 37, 46)
'Gipsy Queen'	Dark purple	Late season	(Plate 8)
'Dr Ruppel'	Striped	Early season	(Plate 66)

It will be equally desirable to have a list of dependable popular Climbing Roses. The dozen below is a combination of the recommendations of The Royal National Rose Society and my own experience.

List of Popular Climbing Roses

Name	Colour	Season	
'Maigold'	Yellow	Early season	(Plate 28)
'Albertine'	Pink	Early season	(Plate 41)
'Zephirine Drouhin'	Pink	Early & continuous	(Plate 34)
'Handel'	Cream, edged pink	Mid season	(Plate 61)
'Schoolgirl'	Orange	Mid season	(Plate 60)
'Golden Showers'	Yellow	mid & continuous	(Plate 59)
'Mermaid'	Yellow	mid & continuous	(Plate 30)
'Compassion'	Pink & apricot	mid & continuous	(Plate 32, *passim*)
'Pink Perpétue'	Pink & carmine	mid & continuous	(Plates 43, 46)
'Parkdirektor Riggers'	Deep Red	mid & continuous	(Plate 67)
'New Dawn'	White & pink	Continuous	(Plate 20)
'Galway Bay'	Glowing pink	Continuous	(Plate 42)

It should be noted that a combination of just 12 roses with 12 clematis offers a combination of 144 plants. Probably more than enough for most gardeners!

TWELVE EASY COMBINATIONS

1. 'Maigold' and 'Lasurstern'   Early season
2. 'Meg' and 'John Warren'   "
3. 'Madame Grégorie Staechelin' and 'Miss Bateman'   "
4. 'New Dawn' and 'Twilight'   Mid season
5. 'Schoolgirl' and 'Prince Charles'   "
6. 'Mermaid' and 'Perle d'Azur'   "
7. 'Parkdirektor Riggers' and 'John Huxtable'   "
8. 'Compassion' and 'Little Nell'   "
9. 'Pink Perpétue' and 'Gipsy Queen'   Late season
10. 'Casino' and 'Victoria'   "
11. 'Golden Showers' and 'Ascotiensis'   "
12. 'Galway Bay' and 'Huldine'   "

*The following chapters present a more detailed account of growing clematis with roses in the five ways listed earlier which are:
Growing clematis with roses BEFORE the rose flowers
Growing clematis with roses WHEN the rose flowers
Growing clematis with roses AFTER the rose flowers
Growing clematis UNDER roses
Growing clematis NEAR roses

CHAPTER THREE
Clematis on Climbing Roses
Before the Roses Flower

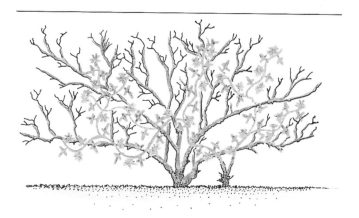

Figure 9. Before the rose flowers it is used as a support for flowering clematis.

This can apply to all roses, whatever their flowering period, as some clematis will flower before them. The idea here is to use the roses before they flower as a support and background to the clematis. The foliage of the rose trees comes to life with the colour given by the clematis (see Plate 51).

THE ROSES

Main Crop Roses
The main crop of roses flowers late enough to allow three groups of clematis to embellish it before the flowers appear.

Examples of popular main crop Climbing Roses are:-
'Albéric Barbier', 'Casino', 'Compassion', 'Danse du Feu', 'Dublin Bay', 'Emily Gray', 'Galway Bay', 'Golden Showers', 'Guinée', 'Handel', 'Climbing Iceberg',

PLATE 51. Alpina 'Constance' of the Alpina Group is a prolific bloomer from mid spring onwards and is ready to clothe a rose with colour.

'Kiftsgate', 'Leverkusen', 'Mme Alfred Carrière', 'Mermaid', 'New Dawn', 'Parkdirektor Riggers', 'Paul's Scarlet', 'Pink Perpétue', 'Schoolgirl', 'Summer Wine', 'Swan Lake'. These will be described in the next chapter.

PLATE 52. The Macropetala 'Jan Lindmark' from Sweden climbs readily into roses from mid spring onwards.

Early Flowering Roses

A few, for example, 'Albertine', 'Gloire de Dijon', 'Maigold', 'Meg', 'Mme Grégoire Staechelin' and 'Zephirine Drouhin' flower so early that they are available to match their flowers with those of the Alpina and Macropetala Groups. This matching will also be described in the next chapter.

THE CLEMATIS

Three groups of clematis may be considered for growing with roses before the roses flower. These are:- 1) The Alpina Group 2) The Macropetala Group 3) The Very Early Large Flowering Clematis.

The Alpina Group

These are compact climbers from 6ft. (1.8m.) to 9ft. (2.75m.). They are very hardy, will grow in poor soil and can be planted on north facing walls (see Plates 51 and 54).

The blooms are single bells - about 1½-2in. (4-5cm.) – made up of four tepals which taper to a point. As the flowers mature they may open flat. Inside the flower are petal-like stamens, staminodes (these are abortive and infertile stamens placed between the fertile stamens and the tepals), which are usually a different colour from the tepals and so add to the attractiveness of the bloom. Blooms are followed by attractive seed heads. The leaves are delicate, usually a soft green, and do not overwhelm the rose. They start flowering from mid spring onwards. This means that they bloom early enough to be used on any Climbing Rose.

This group requires no pruning. However, if the growth has spread outside its allotted space on the rose then the plant can be tidied into place after it has flowered.

Herewith a list of Alpina clematis, grouped according to colour.

White/near white

    C. alpina 'Burford White' - white tepals and staminodes.

    C. alpina 'White Columbine' - creamy-white tepals and white staminodes.

Pink/red

    C. alpina 'Constance' - Deep pink tepals. Deep pink and creamy-white staminodes (see Plate 51).

    C. alpina 'Ruby' - Purple-pink tepals and cream staminodes.

Blue/violet

    C. alpina 'Columbine' – Light blue tepals. Creamy-white staminodes.

    C. alpina 'Frances Rivis' - Largest flower of group. Rich blue tepals and white staminodes, slightly suffused with violet.

    C. alpina 'Frankie' - Mauve-blue tepals and creamy-white staminodes.

    C. alpina 'Jacqueline du Pré – Rosy-mauve tepals and powder pink staminodes.

    C. alpina 'Willy' - Pale pink tepals and creamy-white staminodes.

Selection

    If only one plant is required - *C. alpina* 'Frances Rivis'.

    If three required - 'Burford White', 'Constance', and 'Frances Rivis'.

The Macropetala Group

Although similar to the Alpinas in many respects, they differ in having longer, sometimes protruding staminodes, thus giving an impression of a double rather than a single bell. Some would argue that this quality makes them the more attractive plant.

Like the Alpinas they are compact in habit, very hardy, will grow on north facing walls, climb up to 8ft. (2.4m.) and are thus more vigorous than the former.

Their flowering starts just after the Alpinas and also coincides with them. They are in bloom in mid and late spring and are thus early enough to be available to grace any Climbing Rose (see Plate 52).

The seed heads of this group are amongst the best of all clematis.

As with Alpina, no pruning is required but they can be 'tidied' after flowering.

In the list below the Macropetalas are grouped by colour. The type plant, Macropetala, is as showy as any in the group.

White

    C. macropetala 'Snow White' - White tepals and outer staminodes and greenish-white inner staminodes.

    C. macropetala 'White Lady' - White tepals and staminodes.

    C. macropetala 'White Swan' - Creamy-white tepals and thin white staminodes.

Pink

    C. macropetala 'Markham's Pink' - Bright pink tepals and creamy-pink staminodes. A fine plant.

    C. macropetala 'Rosy O'Grady' - attractive rosy-lilac tepals and white staminodes.

Blue/purple
   C. macropetala - Lavender-blue tepals and white inner staminodes. A fine
   plant (see Plate 55).
   C. macropetala 'Jan Lindmark' - Mauve tepals and twisted pale purple
   staminodes. Interesting bloom (see Plate 52).
   C. macropetala 'Maidwell Hall' - Dark mauve tepals and staminodes.

Selection
   If only one plant is required - *C. macropetala* (see Plate 55).
   If three required - *C. macropetala*, 'Jan Lindmark', 'Rosy O' Grady'.

Very Early Large Flowered Clematis
By late spring some of the Large Flowered Clematis are in bloom. They are early
enough to catch most Climbing Roses out of bloom and thus they can have the
green rose foliage to themselves (see Plate 56).

   They are not early enough to have the foliage of the very early Climbing Roses,
listed on pages 58 and 59, to themselves as the latter will already be in flower. Thus, if
used with them, they should match the flower of the rose.

   Suitable Very Early Large Flowered Clematis are listed below by colour. All are
very rewarding clematis and give much pleasure with colour when gardens are drab.

White
   'Dawn' - Attractive pinky-white bloom with edge of pinky-violet. Carmine
   stamens. Compact short plant to 6ft. (1.8m.).
   'Gillian Blades' - Lovely flower of delicate beauty. Pure white tepals with
   crenated margins and violet staining near the edge. Golden stamens. Up to
   8ft. (2.5m.).
   'Miss Bateman' - Outstanding dramatic flowers. White flower with
   conspicuous boss of chocolate-red stamens. Good grower. Early flowers
   may be attractively tinged with green. Second crop later. Up to 8ft. (2.5m.).

Yellow
Of the only four yellowish clematis, three, are available early on.
   'Guernsey Cream' - Large creamy-yellow tepals and pale yellow stamens.
   Free flowering. Blooms may be attractively tinged with green in early flowers.
   Up to 8ft. (2.5m.). Can be grown in semi-shade. The best of the yellows.
   'Moonlight' - Pale creamy-yellow tepals and creamy-yellow stamens. Short
   plant and not vigorous.
   'Wada's Primrose' - Soft primrose tepals and cream stamens. Early flowers
   may be tinged with green. Up to 6ft. (1.8m.). Worth growing.

Pink-red
   'Vino' - Petunia-red, striking flower with yellow-cream stamens.
   Up to 8ft. (2.5m.).
   'Charissima' - Cerise-pink tepals and maroon stamens. Up to 8ft. (2.5m.)

Blue
   'Alice Fisk' - Attractive flowers. Wisteria-blue tepals and purple stamens.
   Up to 8ft. (2.5m.).

PLATE 53. 'Lasurstern', of German origin, is an outstanding example of the Very Early Large Flowered Group popular for its trouble free nature and lovely bloom.

PLATE 54. Alpina 'Rosy Pagoda' cheers up a rose before it flowers.

'Lasurstern' - Outstanding plant for its vigour, trouble free nature and abundance of bloom. Handsome flower with rich, deep mauve/blue tepals and white stamens. Second crop later. Up to 12ft. (3.6m.) (see Plate 53).

Striped

'Barbara Jackman' - Striking flower with crimson boss on petunia-mauve tepals and cream stamens. Vigorous to 8ft. (2.5m.).

'Nelly Moser' - This old favourite still has a prominent place in the garden for its attractive early flowers and vigorous habit. Tepals of pale mauve-pink with carmine bars - very attractive at bud stage. Maroon stamens. To 8ft. (2.5m.). Second crop later. Tends to fade in strong sun but can be grown in semi-shade (see Plate 57).

Double

'Duchess of Edinburgh' - White tepals and cream stamens. Tries to flower so early that blooms are often distorted and green. If it succeeds it can produce a bloom of exceptional beauty.

PLATE 55. 'Macropetala', the type plant of the Macropetala Group, climbs to the top of rose 'New Dawn' before the rose flowers.

PLATE 56. 'Marie Boisselot' of the Early Large Flowered Group climbs into a rose before the latter flowers.

PLATE 57. 'Nelly Moser', a long-time deserved favourite, of the Early Large Flowered Group, climbs with its striped blooms into a rose before the latter flowers.

Selection
   If only one plant is required - 'Miss Bateman'.
   If three required - 'Miss Bateman', 'Lasurstern', 'Nelly Moser'.

USING THE CLEMATIS

With this group, matching the blooms for colour is not a factor. The aim here is simply to match the clematis flower to the green leaves of the rose, bearing in mind the height and habit of each. Any clematis can be used on any rose.

It must be appreciated that these clematis will always stay on the rose bush as they are not subject to hard pruning. But none are so robust as to interfere with the appreciation of the blooms of the Climbing Roses when they appear later.

The more popular roses and clematis have been used here for illustration. Using the general principles outlined will, however, allow the experienced gardener to extend his choice of roses and clematis.

SUGGESTED PARTNERSHIPS

'Miss Bateman'	on	'Compassion'
'Lasurstern'	on	'New Dawn'
'Macropetala'	on	'Pink Perpétue'
'Frances Rivis'	on	'Golden Showers'
'Guernsey Cream'	on	'Climbing Iceberg'
'Barbara Jackman'	on	'Schoolgirl'

CHAPTER FOUR
Clematis on Climbing Roses
When the Roses Flower

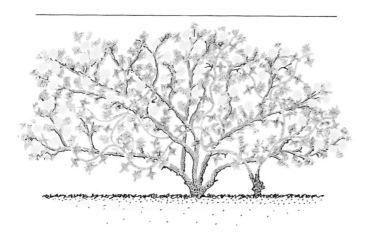

Figure 10. Roses and clematis flower at the same time giving an opportunity for matching their colours

The main crop of roses will coincide with the main crop of Early Large Flowered Clematis.

THE ROSES

The roses to be considered are:

1. The main crop of Climbing Roses. Some will flower once. Some will have two crops. A few are almost continuous flowering.
2. A few are very early flowering roses.

Main Crop Climbing Roses

There are a very large number and it is, therefore, necessary to be selective or the reader will be confused. Those selected here are varieties known to the author and

PLATE 58. 'Perle d'Azur' can flower early enough to be a companion for rose 'New Dawn'.

PLATE 59. 'Golden Showers' is a very popular yellow rose.

in the top twenty of the most popular Climbing Roses in the 1994 Rose Analysis of the Royal National Rose Society. To the Rose Society's list has been added the author's selection of three to boost yellows - 'Casino', 'Emily Gray' and 'Mermaid', one to boost the pinks, 'Galway Bay' and two reds, 'Guinée' and 'Parkdirektor Riggers'. They are grouped here according to their predominant colour.

White/cream

'Albéric Barbier' - Old popular rose from 1900. Very vigorous to 15ft. (4.5m.). Attractive yellow buds opening into flat cream/white flower. Fragrant. One blooming. Dark glossy foliage. Can have mildew.
Needs a strong, tall clematis to match its vigour. All colours, especially mauve/blue, with the exception of white are suitable. Perfect green background for clematis after it has flowered.
'Iceberg' - Climbing. Sport of Floribunda of same name. Vigorous to 10ft. (3m.). Well shaped, double, slightly fragrant blooms suitable for cutting. Susceptible to mildew. Repeat flowering.
Can match any colour of clematis other than creamy/white.
'Kiftsgate' (Rosa filipes) - Enormous, wide growing, rampant plant up to 30ft. (9.2m.) and beyond. Suitable for old deciduous tree or conifer. Prolific bloomer with clusters of small creamy-white fragrant blooms in midsummer. No pruning. Blooms too far away to match clematis. Bottom 6-10ft. (1.8-3m.) may be free of bloom and can be used to support clematis so that the latter covers this bare area. Therefore, can be used before, during or after the rose has bloomed. There is, therefore, a wide choice of clematis (not Montanas which can be too vigorous even for 'Kiftsgate' but can be grown as neighbours).
'Mme Alfred Carrière' - Old favourite from 1879. Vigorous to 20ft. (6.1m.). Very fragrant white, flushed pink, double blooms. Will grow on a north wall. Repeat flowering to some extent.
Can be used with any clematis, especially the more vigorous, of any colour other than creamy/white.
'New Dawn' - Vigorous to 12ft. (3.7m.). White and shell pink, attractive small flower, suitable as a buttonhole flower. Fragrant. A continuous

PLATE 60. Rose 'Schoolgirl' brings clematis 'Victoria' to life with its glowing yellow and orange.

bloomer. Very late blooming if pruned in late summer. Outstanding rose for wealth and quality of bloom, healthy continuous blooming and can be planted anywhere. Runner-up at the International Competition, New Zealand 1994.

Perfect foil for all clematis other than white/cream clematis (see Plate 58).

Orange/yellow

'Casino' - Has fine, large, well-shaped, deep yellow blooms. Not for a harsh climate. Climbs to 10ft. (3m.). Slightly fragrant. Repeat flowering.

Fine companion for all vigorous blue/mauve clematis, especially 'Victoria'.

'Emily Gray' - Not over vigorous – to 15ft. (4.5m.). Unique, fragrant, buff-yellow, well-shaped buds - suitable as button hole. Very fine foliage. One flowering in midsummer. Needs extra care but flowers are unique. Can be liable to mildew. Light pruning.

Fine match for mauve/blue clematis in midsummer.

'Golden Showers' - One of the most popular yellow Climbers (see Plate 59). Has to be encouraged to climb and will reach 7ft. (2.1m.). Bright yellow, fragrant blooms. Continuous flowering. Suitable for small garden.

Excellent choice for matching all the blue/mauve clematis, especially the less vigorous plants.

'Mermaid' - All judgements are subjective but to the author this is the finest Climbing Rose of all. Patience is required as slow to make a large plant – can take four to five years. Ultimately makes a very large plant up to 25ft. (7.6m.) and an awesome sight in bloom. Continuous blooming. Fine foliage. Single, very beautiful, fragrant primrose-yellow blooms - arguably the most attractive rose bloom. Thorns are dreadful. Stems are brittle.

Superb with rich blue or light blue clematis. Unforgettable with 'Perle d'Azur' (see Plate 44).

'Schoolgirl' - Grows to 10ft. (3m.). Attractive double apricot/orange fragrant blooms. Repeat flowering. Continuous blooming.

Matches all mauve/blue and pink clematis (see Plate 60).

PLATE 61. 'Handel' is an eye-catching rose that continues as a favourite for its unusual but attractive, bloom.

Pink

'Compassion' - If you can only have one Climbing Rose then this is it. Vigorous to 15ft. (4.5m.). Beautifully shaped, rosy salmon, shaded apricot bloom. Very fragrant. Repeat flowering until frosts set in. With constant encouragement will cover wall. Flourishes on a north wall. Healthy.
Harmonises well with pink and white clematis as well as mauve/blue clematis.
'Galway Bay' - Vigorous to 10ft. (3m.). Exceptionally large blooms in clusters of glowing deep pink. Slightly fragrant. Repeats and last crop can be in mid autumn.
Matches white and deep mauve clematis.
'Pink Perpétue' - Vigorous to 8ft. (2.5m.). Well-shaped rose and carmine-pink blooms in clusters have a glowing iridescence. Healthy. Productive. Slightly fragrant. Continuous flowering into late autumn.
Mauve/blue clematis pick up the iridescence in rose bloom and are an exceptional match for these clematis (see Plate 62).
'Summer Wine' - If you cannot wait for the single blooms of 'Mermaid' then this is a fine pink alternative. Beautiful flower of coral pink with yellow shading and red stamens. Vigorous to 10ft. (3m.). Repeats. Healthy.
Good companion for white and mauve/blue clematis.

Red

'Dublin Bay' - Rich, deep red double bloom, with slight fragrance. Glossy foliage. Popular, despite reluctance to climb and tendency to remain a shrub. Fine flower but disappointing habit.
Looks good with white clematis.
'Guinée' - You will like or hate the velvety black/red blooms of this rose. Fine bloom with deep fragrance. Vigorous to 15ft. (4.5m.). One good crop in midsummer.
Matches white or light violet/blue clematis.

PLATE 62. 'General Sikorski', a member of the Early Large Flowered Group, is regarded as the finest introduction of the last thirty years and is an excellent match for rose 'Pink Perpétue'.

    'Parkdirektor Riggers' - Vigorous to 15ft. (4.5m.). Deep red semi-double flowers borne in clusters and in profusion. Repeat flowering but dead heading helps. Will grow up a north facing wall (see Plate 67).
    Good companion for white and light mauve/blue clematis.

Bicolour
    'Handel' - A popular rose for its unusual and attractive blooms. Vigorous to 10ft. (3m.). Cream petals with rosy pink edges. Double flowers. Makes an appealing button hole. Repeat flowering.
    A good match for white, pink and mauve/blue clematis but the rose tends to steal the show (see Plate 61).

Selection
    If only room for one - 'Compassion'.
    If only room for three - 'Compassion', 'New Dawn', 'Pink Perpétue'.
    If only room for six - 'Compassion', 'New Dawn','Pink Perpétue', 'Handel', 'Golden Showers', 'Mermaid'.

Early Flowering Roses

It was noted in the last chapter that a few Climbing Roses flower so early that they are in flower before the Very Early Large Flowered Clematis appear and are not available to give them support. However, the two groups, the Alpinas and the Macropetalas, flower so early that they can use even the earliest flowering Climbing Roses for support. In this event the Alpinas and Macropetalas can match the colour of these early roses. Very early flowering, popular Climbing Roses include: 'Albertine', 'Gloire de Dijon', 'Maigold', 'Meg', 'Mme Grégoire Staechelin', 'Zephirine Drouhin'. These are described below with suggestions on matching. All are scented.

Yellow

'Gloire de Dijon' - Wonderful old rose introduced in 1853.
Double bluff-orange coloured, sweetly scented, quartered bloom. Grows to 12ft. (3.6m.). Small blooming later.
Can be matched with pink and blue Alpinas and Macropetalas.
'Maigold' - Vigorous to 12ft. (3.6m.). Attractive light bronze-yellow flaked with pink bloom. Fragrant. Fine clean healthy foliage. Very few blooms after first flush. Thorny stems.
Match with blue/mauve Alpinas and Macropetalas.

Pink

'Albertine' - Vigorous to 15ft. (4.5m.). Double pink, very fragrant bloom. One of the best roses for a vivid display. Liable to mildew.
Almost too covered with bloom to support a clematis as well but the white and blue Alpinas and Macropetalas are suitable.
'Meg' - Pink and apricot attractive blooms in clusters. Fragrant. Grows to 12ft. (3.6m.). A few blooms later.
Match with blue/mauve and white Alpinas and Macropetalas.
'Madame Grégoire Staechelin' - Large bedding type bloom of pink suffused with crimson. Grows to 20ft. (6.1m.) and a very fine sight in bloom. Very fragrant. Rain may cause the large blooms to droop.
Match with blue/mauve Alpinas and Macropetalas on lower parts.
'Zephirine Drouhin' - A thornless old rose - from 1868. Vigorous to 12ft. (3.6m.). Carmine-pink, double blooms. One of the most attractive fragrances. Liable to mildew. Produces flushes of blooms later.
Match with blue/mauve Alpinas and Macropetalas.

Foliage of all, except 'Zephirine Drouhin' which repeats. Available after early blooming as a host for clematis.

Selection

If only one can be grown - 'Maigold'.
If only three can be grown - 'Maigold', 'Meg', 'Zephirine Drouhin' (see also page 59).

THE CLEMATIS

The group of clematis to be considered are:
The Early Large Flowering Clematis that flower in late spring, early summer,

PLATE 63. 'Lasurstern' a vigorous member of the Early Large Flowered Group, is a companion of Mrs. Sam McGredy, a beautiful scented Climbing Rose.

and midsummer are amongst the largest blooming and conspicuous of clematis (see Plate 63). They flower on growth made the previous year and thus are only lightly pruned in early spring. This means that they remain on the rose throughout the year.

Some of the Very Early Large Flowered Clematis mentioned in the last chapter may extend their blooming to this period. They are susceptible to wilt but will respond to the precautions described later (see Chapter 12).

It cannot always be predicted when a climber flowers. Some of the Viticellas, for example, described in the next chapter may flower during this period and can be used for matching.

The clematis described here belong to what at one time were termed clematis of the *Patens, Florida,* and *Lanuginosa* Groups. This nomenclature is not used any longer because extensive hybridising has crossed the boundaries between them.

This group are susceptible to wilt and the antifungal care described later is required. The clematis listed here are of tried reliability, are readily available and will give the gardener a start on which he can build. Fellow gardeners will recommend their favourites and may even give or trade a plant.

The clematis are listed alphabetically by their predominant colour.

White
    'Edith' - Pure white tepals and deep red stamens. Free flowering. Low growing - up to 6ft. (1.8m.).
    'Fair Rosamond' - White tepals with tinge of violet. Purple stamens. Moderately vigorous up to 8ft. (2.5m.). Only Large Flowered Clematis with real perfume - scent of violets.
    C. florida 'Alba Plena' - Striking flower of six white cream tepals with boss of greenish-white staminodes which open to make a double flower. Up to

PLATE 64. 'Niobe', if lightly pruned, flowers early with the Early Flowered Group and can claim to be one of the most popular red clematis.

8ft. (2.5m.). Tender. Not easy to grow. Winter protection on a sheltered wall is necessary. Long lasting flowers.

C. florida 'Bicolor' - (Syn. *C. florida* 'Sieboldii') - as above but with striking maroon-purple staminodes. 'Miss Bateman' is almost as striking and far easier to grow.

'Henryi' - Creamy-white tepals with brown stamens. Vigorous to 10ft. (3m.). A fine old clematis.

'Marie Boisselot' - (Syn. 'Mme Le Coultre') - Pure white tepals and pale yellow stamens. Very vigorous up to 16ft. (4.8m.) A continuous bloomer. The best white clematis. Spread it out so that it does not swamp the rose (see Plate 65).

'Snow Queen' - Recent introduction from New Zealand. White tepals with edge of violet and crenated margins. Deep burgundy stamens. Vigorous to 8ft. (2.5m.). A fine plant.

Yellow

'Lemon Chiffon' - Tinged yellow tepals and yellow stamens. Up to 8ft. (2.5m.).

Pink/red

'Anna' - Introduction from Sweden. Pearly-pink tepals with deeper bar and maroon stamens. Low growing up to 6-8ft. (1.8-2.5m.).

'Barbara Dibley' - Petunia-red tepals with wavy margins and central red bar. Almost a striped clematis. Moderately vigorous to 8ft. (2.5m.).

'John Warren' - Rich cerise-pink pointed tepals and brown stamens. Moderately vigorous to 6ft. (1.8m.).

'Jackmanii Rubra' - Velvety crimson tepals with cream stamens. Continuous flowering. Very vigorous to 20ft. (6.1m.). Pruning optional.

'Niobe' - Velvety ruby-red tepals and golden stamens. Almost black when it first opens. Flowers continuously. Pruning optional. Competes with 'Rouge Cardinal' as the best red. Vigorous to 8ft. (2.56m.). Outstanding (see Plate 64).

'Peveril Pearl' - Attractive pink/lilac tepals with cream stamens. Up to 8ft. (2.5m.).

'Sunset' - New introduction from USA. Showy flower. Velvety red tepals with dark purple blush on petal edges. Golden stamens. Up to 10ft. (3m.).

PLATE 65. 'Marie Boisselot' a beautiful white of the Early Large Flowered Clematis, is a companion for rose 'Compassion'.

'Vino' - Petunia-red tepals with creamy-yellow stamens. Very free flowering.

Blue/purple

'Elsa Späth' - (Syn. 'Xerxes') - Lavender tepals and reddish-purple stamens. Vigorous to 7ft. (2.1m.).

'Fujimusume' - Fine new introduction. Bright blue tepals and cream stamens. Continuous flowering. Vigorous to 12ft (3.6m).

'General Sikorski' - Mid-blue crenated attractive flower, golden stamens. Vigorous to 8ft. (2.5m.). Regarded as best introduction of last twenty years. Spoilt only by tendency to wilt.

'H. F. Young' - Wedgwood blue tepals and creamy-white stamens. Vigorous to 12ft. (3.6m.). Very popular. One of the best blues.

'Lawsoniana' - Old favourite. Lavender-blue tepals have rosy tinge. Beige stamens. Very vigorous to 12ft. (3.6m.). Best choice for very tall clematis. Very large blooms. Long blooming.

'Mrs Cholmondeley' - Lavender-blue tepals and brown stamens. Rather gappy flower. Very popular for its reliability and continuous flowering.

'Richard Pennell' - Rosy-purple tepals and golden stamens. Vigorous to 8ft. (2.5m.). Popular for attractive flower, reliability and continuous flowering.

'Royal Velvet' - A velvety rich, red-purple flower. A new introduction. Likes sun and then vigorous to 8ft. (2.5m.)

COLOUR PLATE 66. 'Dr Ruppel' from Argentina is the most popular striped clematis and is a member of the Early Large Flowered Group.

'The President' - Old favourite. Deep purple tepals and reddish-purple stamens. Vigorous to 10ft. (3m.). Continuous flowering.

'W. E. Gladstone' - Lilac-blue tepals and purple stamens. Dislikes winter and may disappear into soil only to reappear in spring. Has just time to produce enormous blooms - the largest of all.

Striped

'Anna Luise' - A very new introduction with striking flower. Purple tepals with deep red bar. Maroon-red stamens open to reveal white filaments. All combining to make an impact. Vigorous to 10ft. (3m.).

'Bees Jubilee' - An improved 'Nelly Moser' but less vigorous. Lovely flower.

'Fireworks' - A recent introduction. Light purple tepals with broad maroon-red bar and dark stamens which open to reveal white filaments. Vigorous plant to 8ft. (2.5m.). Large bloom.

'Dr Ruppel' - Rose madder tepals with brilliant carmine bar and golden stamens. Vigorous to 10ft. (3m.). Profuse flowering. Very reliable. Very popular and probably best striped clematis (see Plate 66).

'Mrs N. Thompson' - Deep violet-blue tepals with vivid scarlet bar and deep red stamens. A gorgeous bloom but a weak grower to a few feet. 'Star of India' is a stronger alternative plant but flowers later.

'Sealand Gem' - Pale lavender-blue tepals with carmine band. Vigorous to 8ft. (2.5m.). Reliable.

Doubles

Found in early season only. Usually produces a single bloom in early autumn.

'Arctic Queen' - Double white flowers on old and new wood, yellow stamens. Up to 6-8ft. (1.8-2.5m.). A fine new introduction.

'Daniel Deronda' - Violet-blue tepals and cream stamens. A proven favourite. Moderately vigorous to 8ft. (2.5m.).

PLATE 67. Clematis 'Victoria' catches rose 'Galway Bay' in bloom.

'Louise Rowe' – Unusual clematis in that it can present with single, semi-double and double flowers at the same time. White tepals with violet tinge and golden stamens. Not vigorous. Needs special care but worth growing for unusual presentation.

'Jackmanii Alba' - White tepals and brown stamens. Continuous flowering to early autumn. Strong grower to 20ft. (6.1m.).

'Multi blue' - A recent introduction. A sport of 'The President' discovered in Holland. Attractive flower. Tepals in varying shades of blue/purple with blue tips. Opens layer by layer - about a layer a day. Moderately vigorous to 8ft. (2.5m.).

'Proteus' - Rose/lilac tepals and yellow stamens. Peony-like flower. Moderately vigorous to 8ft. (2.5m.). Single blooms later (see Plate 89).

'Royalty' - Rich purple/mauve tepals and yellow stamens. Moderately vigorous to 6ft. (2.1m.).

'Sylvia Denny' - Clear white tepals and yellow stamens. Vigorous to 8ft. (2.5m.).

'Veronica's Choice' - Lavender, crimply tepals. Attractive flower. Moderately vigorous to 8ft. (2.5m.).

'Vyvyan Pennell' - At its best the most attractive flower of all. Truly the Queen of the Clematis. A kaleidoscope of shades of blue/purple. Peony-type bloom. Alas! Particularly liable to wilt. Needs careful antifungal treatment, as described later. Worth the extra care.

Selection

If only one can be grown - 'Mrs Cholmondeley'.

If three plants can be grown - 'Mrs Cholmondeley', 'Marie Boisselot', 'Dr Ruppel'.

If six plants can be grown - 'Mrs Cholmondeley','Marie Boisselot', 'Dr Ruppel', 'Niobe', 'Henryi', 'General Sikorski'.

USING THE CLEMATIS

Matching the colour of the blooms is the vital factor here. Thus we need to consider the colour principles outlined earlier (see pages 46-53). We need also to take account of the height and habit of the clematis and roses (see lists of each here).

It should be noted that the clematis will remain on the roses all the year as these Early Flowering Clematis are not hard pruned. As the Early Large Flowered are not as vigorous as the Late Large Flowered this is not usually a problem.

SUGGESTED PARTNERSHIPS

'Maigold'	with	'Macropetala' (2-3 plants)
'Meg'	with	'Frances Rivis'
'Pink Perpétue'	with	'General Sikorski'
'Handel'	with	'Mrs Cholmondeley'
'Parkdirektor Riggers'	with	'Richard Pennell'
'Schoolgirl'	with	'The President'

CHAPTER FIVE
Clematis on Climbing Roses
After the Roses Flower

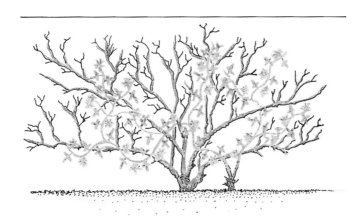

Figure 11. After the rose has flowered it is used as a support for flowering clematis

This arrangement is possible because the clematis tends to flower later and longer than some roses. Other rose blooms may remain, however, especially in the continuous blooming roses, and may put out sporadic blooming right into the late autumn; good examples are 'Compassion', 'Galway Bay', 'Handel', 'New Dawn', and 'Pink Perpétue'. Here it is still possible to match flower with flower although most roses will be bare of flowers and ready to receive colour from clematis.

THE ROSES

The groups of roses to be considered are:

All Climbing Roses.
The very early blooming Climbing Roses become available in early summer while the main crop roses follow at intervals. The roses have been described on pages 65-70.

THE CLEMATIS

The groups of clematis to be considered are:

The Late Large Flowered Clematis Group.
Some can flower very late, for example, 'Lady Betty Balfour', 'Madame Baron Veillard' and 'Ville de Lyon'. An autumn crop from the doubles mentioned earlier can flower alongside this group; these are single blooms, for example, 'Daniel Deronda', 'Proteus', 'Vyvyan Pennell'.

The Viticella Group.

PLATE 68. 'Huldine' is very popular for its clear white colour and being as interesting underneath for its attractive bars. Vigorous, it climbs readily into roses.

The Late Large Flowered Clematis Group

These are often termed the 'Jackmanii' Group. They are not necessarily derived from *Clematis jackmanii* but are like it in habit.

The clematis in this group flower on growth made in the year of flowering. They should, therefore, be severely pruned in early spring to encourage them to make a large quantity of growth and hence a lot of flower (see Plate 69).

In their background there is often Viticella blood. For this reason, probably, they are less susceptible to clematis wilt than the Early Large Flowered Clematis. They can suffer from mildew but this is easily cured (see Chapter 12).

Most grow to a good height. As they have to be hard pruned in the spring of next year anyway, they can be semi-pruned in the autumn to 'tidy up' their appearance on the rose.

In a normal year, most will flower in late summer and early autumn.

Their long stems can be brought down to the ground and they will propagate by layering and serpentine layering as described later.

Again, reliable, readily available clematis are recommended here. They are listed alphabetically according to the predominant colour.

White

'Huldine' - A popular flower. Clear silvery-white tepals. Prominent mauve-purple bar on reverse of tepal, a conspicuous and attractive feature. Vigorous and free flowering up to 15ft. (4.5m.). Can flower late in the season (see Plate 68).
'John Huxtable' - Derived from the very reliable 'Comtesse de Bouchaud'. Pure white tepals and cream-yellow stamens. Vigorous to 8ft. (2.5m.).

Yellow

There are none to be recommended.

Pink/Red

'Allanah' - Fine New Zealand introduction. Bright red tepals. Vigorous to 8ft. (2.5m.).
'Comtesse de Bouchaud' - One of the finest clematis. Moderate size of bloom. Satiny pink tepals with yellow stamens. Very free flowering up to 8ft. (2.5m.). Wilt resistant.
'Ernest Markham' - Bright magenta tepals with reddish-beige stamens. Flowers retain colour. Vigorous to 9ft. (2.7m.)

PLATE 69. *Clematis jackmanii* gives colour to a rose that has finished flowering at The Garden of the Rose, The Royal National Rose Society, St. Albans, U.K. This garden has the world's largest collection of joint planting of roses and clematis.

'Hagley Hybrid' - Probably the most reliable of all Large Flowered Clematis. Easy to grow. Very resistant to wilt. Lovely shell pink bloom when it opens. Brown stamens. Free flowering up to about 6ft. (1.8m.).

'Madame Baron Veillard' - Very late flowering and therefore valuable for this quality. Rosy-pink tepals and white stamens. Vigorous and free flowering up to 15ft. (4.5m.). Grow in a sunny spot as it flowers late.

'Madame Edouard André' - Wine-red tepals and cream stamens. Up to 7ft. (2.1m.). Popular.

'Margaret Hunt' - Clear mauve-pink tepals and brown stamens. Continuous and free flowering. Vigorous to 12ft. (3.6m.). A fine trouble free plant.

'Pink Fantasy' - Pink tepal with brown bar and beige stamens. Low grower to 6ft. (1.8m.).

PLATE 70. 'Madame Julia Correvon' of the Viticella Group is available to cheerfully clothe any flowered rose or match the bloom of continuous flowering roses.

PLATE 71. 'Margot Koster' of the Viticella Group has a long flowering period and brings bright colouring to flowered roses for a long period.

'Rouge Cardinal' - Competes with 'Niobe' as the best red. Dark velvety red tepals and creamy stamens. Low grower to 7ft. (2.1m.).

'Ville de Lyon' - A late flowerer. Carmine tepals with dark tips. Creamy stamens. Reliable. Needs sun. Free flowering to 9ft. (2.7m.).

'Voluceau' - Petunia-red tepals with yellow stamens. Continuous flowering. Vigorous to 12ft. (3.6m.).

Blue/purple

'Ascotiensis' - Flowers late. A fine clean bloom. Reliable. Lavender blue tepals and creamy-green stamens. Vigorous to 12ft. (3.6m.).

'Blekitny Aniol' (Blue Angel) - A recent promising introduction. Pale violet crêpe-like tepals and greeny-yellow stamens. Vigorous to 12ft. (3.6m.). Rivals 'Perle d'Azur' and 'Prince Charles'.

'Lady Betty Balfour' - Very late bloomer with large flower. Needs sunny position. Violet-blue tepals and yellow stamens. Vigorous to 20ft. (6.1m.). Reliable.

PLATE 72. 'Rubra', of the Viticella Group, covers a rose with vivid red blooms after the rose has finished flowering.

PLATE 73. 'Venosa Violacea' of the Viticella Group climbs into rose 'Mme Grégoire Staechelin' after the latter has finished flowering.

'Lilacina Floribunda' - Attractive clear bloom, rich purple with dark stamens. Vigorous to 10ft. (3m.).

'Madame Grange' - Reliable bloomer. Maroon-purple tepals and beige stamens. Very vigorous to 10ft. (3m.).

'Gipsy Queen' - Often found in nurseries sold as either 'Jackmanii' or 'Jackmanii Superba' - as presumably more reliable. The Jackmaniis have a light centre - greenish. 'Gipsy Queen' has a dark centre - reddish-purple. Plum-purple tepals. Very vigorous. Up to 12ft. (3.6m.). Very popular.

'Perle d'Azur' - Most popular of all clematis. Light violet tepals and greenish stamens. Long internodes. Very large plant once established. Very free flowering and vigorous up to 16ft. (4.8m.). A gem.

'Prince Charles' - Rivals 'Perle d'Azur'. Light violet tepals and green stamens. More compact than 'Perle d'Azur'. Very free flowering up to 8ft. (2.5m.)

'Twilight' - Attractive fluorescent clean flower. Petunia-mauve tepals and yellow stamens. Moderately vigorous to 8ft. (2.5m.).

'Victoria' - A neglected very fine clematis. Very reliable and good for a cold climate. Rosy-purple tepals and buff stamens. Very vigorous and free flowering to 16ft. (4.8m.). Its lighter flowers make it a more attractive plant than 'Gipsy Queen' and 'Jackmanii'. Makes a fine partner of either. Highly recommended.

Striped

'Star of India' - One of the most attractive blooms and on an easy-to-grow plant! Tepals a rich velvety, plummy red with a distinct red bar and yellow stamens. Vigorous and free flowering to 20ft. (6.1m.). Deserves more popularity.

Doubles – There are none.

Selection

If only one can be grown - 'Perle d'Azur'.

If only three can be grown - 'Perle d'Azur', 'Hagley Hybrid', 'Victoria'.

If six can be grown - 'Perle d'Azur', 'Hagley Hybrid', 'Victoria', 'Huldine', 'Rouge Cardinal', 'Gipsy Queen'.

The Viticella Group (the purple Virgin's Bower; a small vine.)

This is an outstanding group of clematis from southern Europe that should be grown in every garden. They are very vigorous, hardy and disease resistant. They produce a very large number of medium-sized flowers - though some can approach the Large Flowered Clematis in size. Height to 12ft. (3.6m.) Flowers are bell or saucer-shaped; 1½-2½in. (4-6cm.). Four tepals. In a normal year they flower midsummer to mid autumn.

Varieties:

'Abundance' - Striking pink-red sepals with creamy-green stamens.

'Alba Luxurians' - Creamy-white sepals with green tips and creamy-green stamens. Unusual.

'Betty Corning' - Pale lavender-blue, bell-like flowers. Long flowering period. Scented. From USA.

'Blue Belle' - Very vigorous. Flower is mauve rather than blue.

'Brocade' - Light red flower.

'Campaniflora' - Native of Portugal. Small bell-shaped white flowers tinged with violet. Very vigorous.

'Elvan' - Warm purple colour with creamy-white central bar.

'Etoile Violette' - Large blooms, purple sepals and creamy-yellow stamens. Rivals Jackmanii.

'Grandiflora Sanguinea' (syn. Sodertalje) - Dark red, gappy flower. Very vigorous.

'Little Nell' - Creamy-white. Vigorous. With violet edging.

'Madame Julia Correvon' - Vigorous. Wine-red sepals and golden stamens. Large blooms. Very popular (see Plate 70).

'Margaret Koster' - Mauve-pink sepals and white stamens. Long flowering period (see Plate 71).

'Mary Rose' - Dark mauve. Double. Small flowers in a mass.

'Minuet' - White flower bordered with pinky-mauve edge. Very attractive.

'Polish Spirit' - Rich purple-blue flowers. Very vigorous.

'Purpurea Plena Elegans' - Violet-purple double flowers. Make unusual cut flowers.

'Royal Velours' - Reddish-purple flowers and reddish stamens. Velvety sheen.

'Rubra' (Kermesina) - Crimson sepals and brown stamens (see Plate 72).

'Tango' - White flower with crimson veins and crimson bar around edge.

'Venosa Violacea' - One of the largest blooms. White centre of purple veins with dark purple margins; striking against a white wall (see Plate 73).

C. viticella - The original plant and well worth growing. Small deep purple nodding bell with green stamens.

Selection

All are worth considering.

If only one can be grown - 'Etoile Violette'.

If only three can be grown - 'Etoile Violette', 'Madame Julia Correvon', 'Minuet'.

If only six can be grown - 'Etoile Violette', 'Madame Julia Correvon', 'Minuet', 'Little Nell, 'Margot Koster', 'Purpurea Plena Elegans'.

USING THE CLEMATIS

Matching the blooms of the clematis and roses for colour is not a factor here. Height and habit may be a factor. Therefore see the tables on height of roses (Chapter 3) and clematis (Chapter 5).

All these clematis can be pruned off the roses in the autumn to a height of 2-3ft. (61cms-91.5cm.) and discreetly hidden away (Chapter 12).

SUGGESTED PARTNERSHIPS

'Casino'	with	'Victoria'
'Madame Grégoire Staechelin'	with	'Madame Julia Correvon'
'Compassion'	with	'Little Nell'
'Galway Bay'	with	'Huldine'
'New Dawn'	with	'Perle d'Azur'
'Schoolgirl'	with	'Twilight'

CHAPTER SIX
Clematis Growing Under Climbing Roses

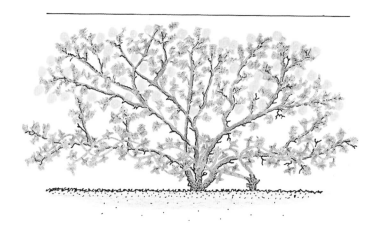

Figure 12. When the Climbing Rose is in or out of bloom the clematis can give colour low down

Clematis can add colour to the garden by using the ground around the rose stem as the lower part of Climbing Roses can be bare. This can be covered by Rockery Clematis in spring while in summer and autumn it can be done with the Texensis and Herbaceous Groups. The rose can be in or out of bloom.

THE ROSES

These are all roses which have been considered on pages 65-70.

PLATE 74.
X durandii, of the Herbaceous Group, can claim to be the most beautiful of all the blue clematis. It is outstanding for its shape, colour, and ease of growing as well as being supreme as a cut flower. Will grow happily under roses.

PLATE 75. *X cartmanii* 'Joe', of the Rockery Group, provides lovely ground cover below roses before the latter flower.

THE CLEMATIS

Suitable clematis groups are:

1. The Rockery Group
2. The Herbaceous Group
3. The Texensis Group

1. The Rockery Group

Clematarians have only developed an interest in this group in recent years. Alpine specialists however, have been interested for many years. The plants are short – from a few in. (cm.) to 2-3ft. (61-91cm.). Most are in flower from mid spring to midsummer. Although suitable for rockeries these plants grow well in a border as long as they have good drainage and are well watered. They can be divided into two sub-sections - New Zealand and American.

New Zealand
All these have separate male and female plants. The male makes the larger flower.

C. marmoraria - The shortest clematis. A gem. A cushion of attractive leaves up to 10in. (25.5cm.) at most. Covered with bloom in spring – creamy-white tinged with green, reminiscent of buttercups. Slow to start and may take three to four years to flower. In very cold areas may need to be grown in pots and the pots put into the ground for the flowering period. The seed heads are spectacular.

C. x *cartmanii* 'Joe' and 'Joanna' - This is a larger plant than the above and covers an area up to 2ft. (61cm.) square. At flowering the plant is covered with pure white or creamy-white flowers – often with an attractive tinge of green. An outstanding plant (see Plate 75).

Hybridists are busy crossing the above with other New Zealand clematis and have produced a number of attractive rockery plants, available from specialist nurseries

American

C. addisonii - Will grow slowly to 20in. (50cm.). A small Texensis type - tubular flower. Reddish-purple exterior.

C. columbiana ssp. *tenuiloba* - Purple Alpina-like flower on a short plant 4-6in. (10-15cm.) high.

C. douglasii var. *scottii* - Deep lavender globular urns on a plant up to 20in. (50cm.).

Other

C. chrysocoma - A dwarf form of the huge plant is becoming available.

2. The Herbaceous Group

As the title implies this is a group of plants whose stems die down in the winter and although they prune themselves, a tidy is still recommended. They can make large plants which in the winter can be divided up into sizes suitable for the gardener's purpose. They can be divided into two sub-sections – *integrifolia* and *heracleifolia*. The former are tidy plants; the latter are larger and coarser. A feature of this group is that they do not use their petioles for climbing and they scramble and clamber. As a consequence, they will get ideal support from the lower portions of the rose.

Integrifolia - Attractive, nodding bell-like flowers are borne on their stems, over a long period of time from early summer to early autumn and the stems may need some support. A large number is now available of different colours:

'Alba' - The white form. Scented.

'Arabella' - A fine new form. Large blue-purple flowers. Cream stamens. Will scramble up to 6ft. (1.8m.). Blooms early summer to mid-autumn.

X durandii - Strong long flowering plant. Has one of the finest blooms in all clematis. Indigo-blue flowers of interesting shape and yellow stamens (see Plates 74 and 77). Can clamber up to 6ft. (1.8m.).

C. eriostemon 'Hendersonii' – Bell-shaped purple flowers over a long period. Up to 6ft. (1.8m.).

'Hendersonii' - Purple-blue.

'Olga' - Mid blue. Scented.

'Pastel Blue' - Light blue. Scented.

'Pastel Pink' - Light pink.

'Petit Faucon' - Unusual deep indigo flower. A fine plant.

'Rosea' - Deep pink colour. One of the finest herbaceous plants in the garden.

'Tapestry' - Mauvy-red. Attractive plant.

Selection

If only one plant can be planted – *X durandii*

If only three plants can be planted – *X durandii*, *C. integrifolia* 'Rosea', 'Petit Faucon'.

Heracleifolia - Makes a large plant from early summer to early autumn.

The leaves are a big feature and drown the small hyacinth-like flower. Often scented.

'Cote d'Azur' - Pale blue flowers. Scented.

'Davidiana' - Lavender-blue scented flowers.

'Edward Prichard' - Not as robust as the others. Pretty flower with good colour. Very scented.

X jouiniana 'Praecox' - The finest scrambling and ground cover clematis. Covers a large area. Profuse production of white flowers with violet margins. Flowers obscure the coarse leaves.

'Mrs Robert Brydon' - Makes the largest plant. Blue and white flowers.

C. recta ' Purpurea' - Panicles of small, white, scented flowers. Makes a fine bush up to 4ft. (1.2m.). Purple-bronze foliage.

'Wyevale' - Blue, scented flowers.

Selection

If only one plant can be planted - *X jouiniana* 'Praecox'.

If only three plants can be planted - *X jouiniana* 'Praecox', 'Edward Prichard', and 'Wyevale'.

3. The Texensis Group

This group contains some of the most attractive clematis flowers - tulips of different shades dancing in the breeze. Each hybrid has its supporters. All are attractive. The plants make a bush up to 6ft. (1.8m.) tall. There are some related plants.

'Duchess of Albany' - A clear pink with rose-pink bars. Cream stamens.

'Etoile Rose' - Wide bell with recurved lips. Cherry-red colour with silvery margin (see Plate 78).

'Gravetye Beauty' - Rich ruby-red colour of tepals with red stamens.

'Lady Bird Johnson' - Dusky-red colour.

'Sir Trevor Lawrence' - Crimson interior with cream stamens. Cream and red satiny mixture on the outside. Perhaps the best?

'The Princess of Wales' - Vivid pink colour. Creamy-yellow stamens (see Plate 76).

Related Plants

C. crispa - Attractive purple flowers with recurving edges.

C. fusca - A strange looking flower. The tepals are covered with dark brown hairs. Worth growing as a talking point.

C. simsii - Purple-blue small pitcher-shaped flowers.

C. viorna - Red urn-shaped flower with yellow interior.

Selection

All are so attractive that it becomes a matter of personal preference.

USING THE CLEMATIS

The Rockery Clematis remain on the ground throughout the year and are unobtrusive. If they need protection they can be grown in pots and brought out for the flowering season.

The Herbaceous and Texensis Groups can be semi pruned after flowering to leave a tidy bottom to the rose. The pruning is completed in the early spring.

PLATE 76. The Texensis Group is unsurpassed for elegant companionship below roses. 'The Princess of Wales' has vivid pink colouring.

PLATE 77. *X durandii* of the Herbaceous Group displays its lovely blooms below rose 'Schoolgirl'.

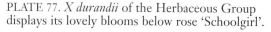

SUGGESTED PARTNERSHIPS

C. marmoraria (several) beneath 'Zephirine Drouhin'
C. integrifolia 'Rosea' (2-3) beneath 'New Dawn'
X durandii beneath 'Schoolgirl'
'Arabella' beneath 'Casino'
C. texensis 'Sir Trevor Lawrence' beneath 'Kiftsgate'
X jouiniana 'Praecox' beneath 'Golden Showers'

PLATE 78. 'Etoile Rose' of the Texensis Group blooms abundantly below a rose at The Garden of the Rose, The Royal National Rose Society, St. Albans, U.K. By the year 2000 it is planned to have a massive expansion in the area of the garden and its display of clematis.

CHAPTER SEVEN
Clematis Near Climbing Roses

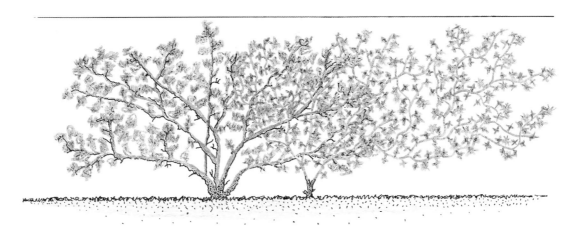

Here the principle is that while roses and clematis would make good companions, the clematis are such strong growers that they would swamp the rose. A few roses would swamp the clematis. Thus the clematis can be planted near but not on the rose. The most obvious common support for the rose and clematis is a wall, trellis, or fence (see Plate 82). They can also be near one another on a pergola, gazebo, or climbing into a tree. They can be on posts close to one another but they must be kept apart.

They may flower to coincide with the roses or they can be used to give colour when roses are unable to provide any of their own.

Figure 13. A clematis can be in bloom near a Climbing Rose which is in or out of bloom

PLATE 79. *Clematis cirrhosa* of the Evergreen Group can be a companion to a rose on a wall and give colour and scent before the rose flowers. The variety 'Freckles' is heavily speckled inside the bloom.

THE ROSES

These have been described on pages 65-70.

THE CLEMATIS

The clematis to be considered, in order of flowering, are:

1. The Evergreen Group
2. The Montana Group
3. The Orientalis Group
4. The Late Species Group.

Two, the Evergreen and Montana Groups, flower from midwinter to late spring. Two, the Orientalis and Late Climbing species flower late in the season - from early to late autumn.

The Evergreen Group

These clematis are the first to flower - as early as early winter. They supply colour, when none is available on the roses and they need no pruning.

There are three sub groups:

1. *Clematis cirrhosa*

    Needs the shelter of a warm wall out of the wind. Is vigorous to 20ft. (6.1m.). The flowers are yellow-white hanging bells and scented (citrus). The foliage is attractive, fern-like and may turn bronze in the winter. The four tepals may be freckled on the inside. *C. cirrhosa* can be in flower from early winter. In addition to the above, common varieties are:

    'Wisley Cream' - with cream flowers and few markings.

    'Freckles' - heavily speckled, red-purple, inside. Scented (see Plate 79).

    'Ourika Valley' - hardy pale yellow flowers. No markings. Flowers late winter to early spring.

2. *Clematis armandii* and related plants

    Flourishes out of the wind on a sheltered wall. Makes a very wide and high plant up to 15ft. (4.5m.) x 15ft. (4.5m.). Large leathery, glossy leaves. Produces clusters of creamy-white flowers – bell-shaped at first and then opening almost flat. Heavily scented. Flowers in early spring. Exceptional, most desirable plant when there is room for it. Varieties are 'Apple Blossom', 'Snowdrift' and 'Jefferies'.

    Related plants are: *C. finetiana, C. x jeuneana, C. meyeniana, C. quinquefoliata, C. uncinata.*

3. New Zealand Border Climbing Clematis

    New Zealand Clematis are commercially divided into Border and Rockery Groups. See previously (pages 85-86) for rockery plants. All have male and female forms but male flowers are the finer.

    C. afoliata (Rush stemmed clematis) Flowers late spring. Interesting untidy plant that needs protection in cold areas. Moderately vigorous to 8ft. (2.5m.). A tubular pale yellow flower. Some fragrance (Daphne scent).

    C. foetida Flowers are chartreuse-green of 5-8 tepals. Strongly scented. Needs protection in cold areas. Vigorous to 20ft. (6.1m.). Flowers late spring.

C. forsteri Flowers early summer. Needs protection in cold climates. Height to 12ft. (3.6m.). Greenish-yellow tepals with golden stamens. Fragrant (lemon).
C. paniculata (syn. *indivisa*) Needs conservatory or sheltered position. Height to 15ft. (4.5m.). Leathery leaves. Lovely flower of pure white tepals and pink stamens. Flowers late spring. A highly desirable plant, given protection.
C. petriei Profuse flowerer. Flowers of six tepals that are yellow-green. Pale green stamens. Needs protection in very cold areas. Flowers late spring. Affinity with *C. forsteri*.

Selection

If there is room, then *C. armandii*, covers a large area, has a fine display of flowers at a dull time of the year and has heavy fragrance.

The Montana Group

The plant, as the name suggests, comes from the mountains. It was first discovered in Nepal and can be found throughout the mountain ranges of India and China. The whites are found in India and the pinks in China.

These are the 'giants' of the clematis world. They are very vigorous, cover a large area and produce flowers in profusion. They are so showy that some gardeners think the clematis year has started here when some fine plants have gone before.

The most vigorous can climb to 30ft. (9.1m.) and beyond. Many are scented. Flowers of four tepals vary in size from 2in. (5cm.) to 3½in. (9cm.).

There are some related plants which are well worth growing.
The Montanas have advantages and disadvantages. They should be grown early in the year for a profuse display of flowers. It is a plant of great vigour and with flowers that are usually scented. They flower, however, for only three to four weeks and in a hard winter the stems are leafless twigs. They are best grown, therefore, with roses not seen from the house as the colour will attract you out of doors to see them in flower. A hard frost can damage or even destroy the flower buds - as happened in the spring of 1990 in the United Kingdom.

The Montanas are divided into four sections – white, pink, double, related.

White

'Grandiflora' - Profuse flowerer. Large bloom with yellow stamens. Usually fragrant.
'Mrs Margaret Jones' - Small flower. Semi-double.
'Wilsonii' - Vigorous. Star-shaped flowers with prominent yellow stamens. Chocolate fragrance. Flowers one month later than most.

Pink

'Elizabeth' - Pale pink, large bloom with yellow stamens. Strongly scented.
'Freda' - Most attractive, cherry-pink flower with deeper pink on margin and golden stamens. Fine coppery foliage. Less vigorous than most and suitable for a small garden. With care can partly climb into a rose (see Plates 80 and 85).
'Mayleen' - Very vigorous and easy to grow. Large bloom with prominent boss of golden stamens. Strongly scented.

PLATE 80. *Clematis montana* 'Freda' is one of the smaller plants of the Montana Group but makes a major impact. Its striking colouring can be edged into a large Climbing Rose.

PLATE 81. *Clematis rehderiana* of the Orientalis Group makes a very large plant. As a companion to a rose on a wall it will give colour and fragrance after most roses have finished blooming. The panicles of pale yellow trumpets have a cowslip scent.

PLATE 82. A number of roses climb over this wall. There is room for a Montana and so *Clematis montana* 'Vera' has been planted half way along the wall beneath the roses.

'Odorata' - Creamy-pink flowers. Vigorous. Bronze foliage. Flowers late. Strong scent.

'Picton's Variety' - Pink bloom. Not vigorous. Little fragrance.

'Reubens' - Very variable in colour and vigour (see Plate 83). Likely to be displaced by 'Fragrant Spring' from Holland.

'Tetrarose' - Large bloom of a deep pink colour with straw-coloured stamens. Not a large plant. Short flowering period. Fine foliage. Likely to be displaced by an even finer plant - 'New Dawn' from Holland.

'Vera' - A very strong grower. Fragrant. Large leaves (see Plate 82).

Doubles

'Broughton Star' - A deep pink. Golden stamens. Free flowering.

'Marjorie' - Creamy-pink with salmony stamens. Not a profuse flowerer. Arouses strong feelings of like or dislike.

Related

C. chrysocoma - Tiny hairs on leaves and stamens. Creamy-white bloom with light pink margins. Less hardy than Montanas but flowers over a longer period. 'Continuity' is a very attractive variety that flowers later and for a longer period but is less hardy.

C. chrysocoma var. *sericea* (syn. 'Spooneri')

Fine, clear, large white flower. Vigorous. No fragrance. A fine plant. Blooms two weeks after Montanas.

C. x *vedrariensis* - A cross between *C. chrysocoma* and a *C. montana* and does not improve on either. Pink flowers. Not vigorous.

Selection

> For a small garden - 'Freda'.
> For a large garden - 'Mayleen' if one required. If three required 'Mayleen', 'Spooneri' and 'Broughton Star'.

The Orientalis Group

This is the group of yellow clematis. This late flowering (late summer and early autumn) group has fine foliage and has the bonus of often spectacular seed heads and being easy to grow. The flowers are attractive lantern-shaped, bell-shaped or an open bell. Can be pruned hard or given no pruning for early flowering.

The classification of this group is complicated but for the gardener it comes down to a few well-described, available garden plants together with some related plants. Plants of medium height - up to 20ft. (6.1m.).

These are taken in alphabetical order below:

> 'Bill Mackenzie' - A fine large plant. Large open bell-shaped flower. Fine seed heads. Due to a long flowering period - midsummer to late autumn - often has flowers and seed heads together. The best of the group.
> *C. orientalis* 'Ludlow & Sherrif' - Botanical background is confused. Generally known as 'Orange Peel' clematis for the four yellow, thick tepals that make it the open bowl type of flower. It has slaty-purple stamens. A short flowering period in mid autumn.
> 'Helios' - A very desirable introduction from Holland. Shorter plant than most in this group. Starts flowering early - in late spring and has long flowering period. Very productive of large light yellow flowers. Ideal over low Shrub Roses and for a small garden.
> *C. tangutica* - Characterised by lantern-shaped, lemon-yellow flowers and large seed heads. Medium height. There are many varieties 'Aureolin', 'Burford', 'Corry', 'Gravetye', 'Lambton Park', etc.

Related Plants

> *C. orientalis* var. *akebioides* - Attractive glaucous leaves. Yellowish-green open flowers. Does not appeal to all.
> *C. ladakhiana* - Attractive fern-like foliage. Yellow star-shaped flowers tending to be lost in the foliage.
> *C. serratifolia* - Interesting alternative to the common Orientalis plants. Pale yellow flowers with purple stamens. Flowers in late summer for short period. Up to 12ft. (3.6m.). A variety from Holland 'Golden Harvest' is desirable.
> *C. rehderiana* - A giant of a plant to 20ft. (6.1m.) covered with panicles of small straw yellow tubular flowers with recurving tips. Strong cowslip scent. Very desirable plant if there is room (see Plate 81).

Selection

> For small garden - 'Helios'
> For medium-sized garden - 'Bill Mackenzie'
> For large garden - The above plus *C. rehderiana*

The Late Species Group

We have here a group of plants that flower in late summer and autumn and not only extend the flowering period of the clematis but of the garden. Most are outstanding for a large display of bloom while some, in addition, are most fragrant.

Some have an affinity to the wild clematis of Europe - *C. vitalba*, and of Australia - *C. aristata* and of the United States - *C. virginiana*. These very vigorous wild clematis can be controlled by growing in a container and an autumn pruning can enhance the display of flowers.

As sun is limited in the autumn they benefit from being grown in sunny places. If necessary all can be hard pruned to control their vigour or just pruned into their allotted place.

They are listed here alphabetically.

C. flammula - A magnificent plant which should be in every garden. Flowers are tiny in the shape of a star with white stamens. The flowers are in panicles. Very abundant production of flowers leads to a cloud effect. Strong hawthorn-like scent. Can make a large plant - up to 20ft. (6.1m.).

C. fargesii - Another large plant - up to 25ft. (7.6m.). The flowers have six white tepals with greenish-white stamens. With no pruning can start flowering in early summer and go on to late autumn. With pruning it starts flowering in midsummer.

C. terniflora - A large plant up to 30ft. (9.1m.). Is meant to be covered with masses of white flowers bearing a hawthorn-like scent. Needs to be in a very sunny position to flower at all.

C. napulensis - Looks like a dead plant throughout the summer. Comes to life with attractive foliage in late autumn. If it flowers, there are clusters of creamy-white bells with purple stamens. Needs warm sheltering wall or conservatory.

C. triternata 'Rubro-marginata' - Derived from *C. flammula* with similar habit. Flower is slightly larger and white flower has purple-red margin and green stamens. Strongly scented. Colour of flower and profusion of flowers makes a most attractive and desirable plant. Another plant for every garden (see Plate 84).

C. 'Western Virgin' - A *vitalba*-like flower from Canada (hence its name 'Prairie Traveller's Joy'). Makes an enormous plant covered with white flowers of 4-6 tepals and long white stamens. Up to 35ft. (106.m.)!

Selection

All gardens – *C. triternata* 'Rubro-marginata' and then find room for *C. flammula*

Large gardens - As above plus *C. fargesii*

USING THE CLEMATIS

The clematis is not on the rose but nearby with its own support. No matching of colour of rose and clematis is required here with the exception of the Orientalis Group, the flowering of which may coincide with that of roses.

The Evergreen and Montana Groups will have flowered before the rose. The

PLATE 83. *Clematis montana* 'Reubens' lives near rose 'Compassion' and has been allowed to edge into the rose to welcome its first blooming.

PLATE 84. Truly a plant for all gardens, *Clematis triternata* 'Rubro-marginata' of the Late Species Group gives colour and fragrance in a rose garden after the roses bloom. The plant is outstanding for its vigour, colouring, fragrance and large size.

PLATE 85. A space near a Climbing Rose has been planted with the not over vigorous *Clematis montana* 'Freda'. It will not be allowed to embarrass the rose.

Late Climbing Species will flower after the rose has flowered.

Only the Orientalis Group will flower at the same time as the rose. There are no blue roses for a perfect match with the yellow Orientalis Group. Here we must make do with an orange or a white.

Useful structures for supporting clematis are discussed later (see Chapter 12).

SUGGESTED PARTNERSHIPS

C. montana 'Mayleen' near 'Kiftsgate'
C. cirrhosa near ' Compassion'
C. armandii near 'Meg'
C. montana 'Freda' creeping into 'Maigold'
C. orientalis 'Bill Mackenzie' on pillar near 'New Dawn' also on pillar.
C. flammula on pillar near 'Galway Bay' on pillar.

SYNCHRONISING GROWING CLEMATIS WITH CLIMBING ROSES

This table summarises the time of the year when growing Climbing Roses and Clematis together can take place.

Column 1 gives the season of the year.

Column 2 summarises what is happening to the Climbing Rose at a given time.

Column 3 tells what clematis groups are available before the roses bloom. It should be used in combination with Columns 1 and 2

Column 4 lists the clematis available when the roses bloom. It should be used in combination with Columns 1 and 2

Column 5 lists the clematis available after the roses bloom. It should be used in combination with Columns 1 and 2

Column 6 lists the clematis available near the rose. It should be used in combination with Columns 1 and 2

Column 7 lists the clematis available beneath the rose and should be used in combination with Columns 1 and 2.

The time periods given are approximate and are those to be expected in an average year. In years when there is more heat than expected the flowering of the clematis will be brought forward and the season shortened. In years when there is more dull weather than usual the flowering of the clematis will be delayed and the season lengthened.

AVAILABILITY OF CLEMATIS FOR CLIMBING ROSES

1 Season	2 Roses	3 Before	4 When	5 After	6 Near	7 Beneath
Early winter	Out of flower				Evergreen	
Mid-winter	Out of flower				Evergreen	
Late winter	Out of flower				Evergreen	
Early spring	Out of flower					
Mid spring	Very early roses in bloom	Alpina Macropetala				Rockery
Late spring	Early roses in flower	V. Early Flowering Clematis			Montana	
Early summer	Main crop in flower		Early Large Flowered	Early Large Flowered		
Mid-summer	Main crop in flower		Early Large Flowered	Early Large Flowered		Texensis Herbaceous
Late	Repeat flowering in bloom		Viticellas Late Large Flowered	Viticellas Late Large Flowered	Orientalis Late Species	Texensis Herbaceous
Early autumn	Some roses in bloom		Viticellas Late Large Flowered	Viticellas Late Large Flowered	Orientalis Late Species	Texensis Herbaceous
Mid autumn	A few in bloom				Late Species	
Late	A few in bloom				Late Species	

PLATE 86. The Shrub Rose 'Lawrence Johnston' is full of colour when it flowers and invites enhancement by clematis.

CHAPTER EIGHT
Clematis With Shrub Roses

This book concentrates on the companionship of Climbing Roses and Clematis. In almost every respect Clematis and the lovely Shrub Roses can be dealt with in the same way.

The Old Shrub Roses are characterised by a burst of overwhelmingly beautiful flowers, often with a gorgeous scent, in the early summer. Thereafter, blooms may be absent or the second floral display small. The Modern Shrub Roses, however, flower with the main group of roses in early and midsummer, some with repeat flowers. Some such as 'Buff Beauty' and 'Felicia', are at their best in the autumn. A special group, the Creeping or Ground Cover Shrub Rose, will be considered with Bedding Roses.

Shrub Roses, with their companion Clematis, can be in a shrubbery devoted entirely to roses - rose shrubbery. The Shrub Roses can also be used with other shrubs as a part of a mixed collection. It is also not unusual to plant the shorter Shrub Roses as a part of an herbaceous border. Formality is giving way to informality in the rose world.

There are great opportunities for matching Shrub Roses with Clematis although, hitherto, they have been greatly neglected. Using Clematis enormously increases the

PLATE 87. The shrub rose 'Canary Bird' makes a colourful combination with Montana 'Rubens' early in the season.

amount of colour in a rose shrubbery and extends the period when colour can be seen.

As with Climbing Roses, Clematis can be planted with the Shrub Rose before, during, or after the shrub has bloomed. They can also be planted near a shrub.

THE SHRUB ROSES

There is a very large selection. In the section entitled 'The Best Roses to Grow as Shrubs', in 1994 The Royal National Rose Society had 147 roses recommended. Seventeen were selected. My selection has been taken from that list together with some selected as 'The Best Old Garden Roses', by the same society; many of these have a shrubby habit. To those I have added one shrub grown for its foliage (*Rosa glauca*). I had a bias towards yellow flowers to match the common blue/mauve clematis. These are not found in the very old Shrub Roses. Size is given in Width x Height.

The Shrub Roses fall into three groups for planning:

1) The Very Early Flowering Shrubs - for example, 'Canary Bird', 'Nevada' and 'Frühlingsgold'. They bloom early on and are therefore available as an early support for clematis.

2) The Mid Season Shrub Roses that flower once. They are available for clematis after the flowering.

3) The Repeat Flowering Shrubs. Clematis used here can be matched with the roses. Twenty Shrub Roses are named here. Three flower very early -'Canary Bird', 'Nevada' and 'Frühlingsgold'. Two can flower very late -'Buff Beauty' and 'Felicia'. The remainder start flowering midsummer and of these the Old Roses will tend not repeat while the Modern Shrub Roses will tend to repeat. The shrubs vary in size from a low shrub (e.g. 'Ballerina') to a medium-sized shrub (e.g. 'Canary Bird') to a large shrub (e.g. 'Frühlingsgold'). The Shrub Roses are listed here alphabetically and by colour groups.

White

'Boule de Neige' - A Bourbon shrub. White ball-like flowers. Very fragrant. Flowers midsummer. Repeats later. Size 5ft. (1.5m.) x 3ft. (91cm.).

'Madame Hardy' - A Damask shrub. Large white double flowers. Fragrant. Flowers midsummer. Size 5ft. (1.5m.) x 4ft. (1.2m.).

'Nevada' - An old favourite shrub of large size. *Moyesii* hybrid. Creamy-white flowers. Little fragrance. Size 7ft. (2.1m.) x 7ft. (2.1m.).

'Sally Holmes' - A modern medium-sized Shrub Rose. Large, single creamy-white blooms. Fragrant. Size 5ft. (1.5m.) x 4ft. (1.2m.).

Pink

'Ballerina' - This is a modern low-growing shrub. Flowers are pink, white and single. Size 3½ft. (1.06m.) x 3ft. (91cm.). Fragrant. Repeat flowering.

'Celestial' - An Alba rose. Double pink blooms. Very fragrant. Flowers midsummer. Size 6ft. (1.8m.) x 4ft. (1.2m.).

'Fantin-Latour' - Centifolia shrub. Large, double, pink blooms. Flowers in midsummer. Fragrant. Size 7ft. (2.1m.) x 7ft. (2.1m.).

'Felicia' - A Hybrid Musk rose of medium size. Double, apricot-pink blooms. Very fragrant. Long flowering period from early summer onwards and often best in the autumn. Size 5ft. (1.5m.) x 7ft. (2.1m.).

'Koenigin von Danemarck' - An Alba shrub. Quartered, crimson-pink flowers. Flowers midsummer. Fragrant. Size 5ft. (1.5m.) x 4ft. (1.2m.).

'Madame Isaac Pereire' - Large, old Bourbon rose. Large, carmine-pink, double flowers. Very fragrant. Flowers midsummer. Size 8ft. (2.4m.) x 6ft. (1.8m.).

'Penelope' - A popular medium-sized Hybrid Musk shrub. Semi-double pale pink flowers. Fragrant. Flowers early summer. Repeats. Size 6ft. (1.8m.) x 6ft. (1.8m.).

Rosa gallica versicolor (Rosa Mundi). Very old Gallica shrub. Stripes all over petals on semi-double blooms. No fragrance. Flowers midsummer. Size 4ft. (1.2m.) x 3ft. (91cm.).

Rosa rubrifolia (Rosa glauca) - A Species Rose grown especially for its foliage

PLATE 88. By the end of July this enormous Shrub Rose is devoid of colour. Using a number of clematis it could be a riot of colour for weeks to come

and hips. Leaves are an attractive purple. Flowers are small and pink. Not fragrant. Size 6ft. (1.8m.) × 6ft. (1.8m.).

Red

'Fred Loads' - A modern, medium-sized Shrub Rose. Single vermilion blooms. Fragrant. Continuous flowering. Size 6ft. (1.8m.) × 4ft. (1.2m.).

Yellow/Orange

'Buff Beauty' - A Hybrid Musk. Medium-sized shrub. Double apricot flowers. Fragrant. Summer and strong autumn flowering. Size 4ft. (1.2m.) × 4ft. (1.2m.).

'Canary Bird' - A Species Rose and a favourite for its early flowering. Single yellow blooms on arching stems. Fragrant. Thorny. Ferny grey-green foliage. Flowers in late spring. Size 6ft. (1.8m.) × 6ft. (1.8m.). May need a support.

'Chinatown' - A modern Shrub Rose (see Plate 87). Fine double yellow blooms edged with pink. Fragrant. Repeat flowering 5ft. (1.5m.) × 4ft. (1.2m.).

'Frühlingsgold' - A large popular Species Rose. Beautiful, large semi-double, creamy-yellow flowers. Fragrant. Flowers early - in late spring. Size 8ft. (2.4m.) × 7ft. (2.1m.).

'Graham Thomas' - A modern medium-sized shrub. Large yellow blooms. Fragrant. Repeat flowering. Size 4ft. (1.2m.) × 4ft. (1.2m.).

Purple

'Roseraie de l'Hay' - A large *rugosa* shrub. Large, velvety, double purple blooms. Fragrant. No hips. Some repeat flowering. Size 7ft. (2.1m.) × 7ft. (2.1m.).

Selection

One shrub rose to be grown - 'Canary Bird'

Three shrub roses to be grown - 'Canary Bird', 'Frühlingsgold', 'Nevada'.

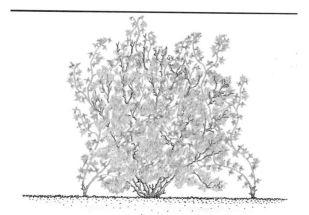

Figure 14. Before the Shrub Rose blooms it can be used as a support by flowering Clematis

Figure 15. The flowering Clematis can climb into a flowering Shrub Rose with an opportunity for matching the colours

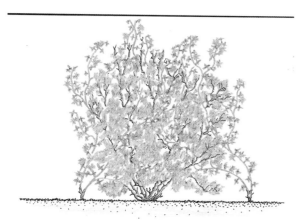

Figure 16. After the Shrub Rose flowers it can be used as a support by flowering Clematis

THE CLEMATIS BEFORE THE ROSES FLOWER

Shrub Roses flower so early that the only suitable clematis likely to flower before them are the Alpinas and Macropetala Groups. See list pages 59-61. Both the Evergreen and Montana groups are early but too vigorous and would prevent the Shrub Roses from flowering.

Both Alpina and Macropetala Groups are suitable on shrubs up to about 6ft. (1.8m.). However, after flowering they will remain on the shrub for the rest of the year as they are not pruned. The Alpinas are less obtrusive than the Macropetalas. If employed then it will not be possible to use the shrubs later to support other clematis as these would swamp the Alpinas or Macropetalas.

THE CLEMATIS WHEN THE ROSES FLOWER

Coinciding with the blooming of Shrub Roses are the Early Large Flowered Clematis. Following the principles of colour matching, suitable combinations can be made with the Modern Shrub Rose. However, there is a possible disadvantage with the Old Shrub Roses. The Old Shrub Roses are uniquely beautiful for a short period and many would argue that they should be enjoyed as they are.

It must be remembered that the Early Large Flowered Clematis are only lightly pruned and will remain on the plant for the rest of the year, including the winter, and can be unsightly.

The scope at this time is limited. If matching is attempted a list of Early Large Flowering Clematis is found on pages 61-62 and 70-76.

THE CLEMATIS AFTER THE ROSES FLOWER

The third option is the best, and offers the possibility of a dazzling display of colour after the shrub has stopped flowering. Furthermore, the clematis used can be pruned off in the autumn so that no unsightly display remains over winter and the shrub can flower in all its glory in spring and summer. This excludes using the Early Large Flowering Clematis. A rich selection of clematis remains.

The following groups of clematis are possibles of which the first two are exceptional.

1. Late Large Flowering Clematis Group. See list pages 78-82.
2. The Viticella Group. See pages 82-83.
3. The Herbaceous Group - See pages 86-87. Of particular suitability are two tall integrifolias - 'Durandii' and 'Arabella'.
4. The Texensis Group. See page 87.
5. The Orientalis Group - See page 94. Some are too vigorous. Suitable are *C. tangutica* and 'Helios'.

THE CLEMATIS NEAR THE SHRUB ROSE

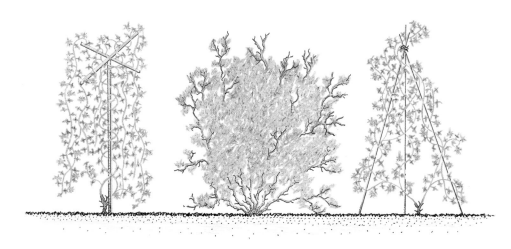

Figure 17. Clematis can be in bloom on a support near a Shrub Rose

A shrubbery or border of Shrub Roses can be very drab before or after flowering. Colour can be added with clematis on the shrub as mentioned above. Colour can also be added by planting clematis on supports between the Shrub Roses. As there is no possibility of swamping the rose, even large clematis can be used. All the groups of clematis can be used in a sequence through the clematis year. The Rockery Group is too short for this purpose.

1. The Evergreen Group. See pages 90-91.
2. The Alpina and Macropetala Groups. See pages 59-61.
3. The Montana Group on large supports. See pages 91-93.
4. The Early Large Flowered Clematis Group. See pages 61-62 and 70-76.
5. The Late Large Flowering Clematis Group. See pages 78-82.
6. The Viticella Group. See pages 82-83.
7. The Herbaceous Group. See pages 86-87.
8. The Texensis Group. See page 87.
9. The Orientalis Group. See page 94.
10. The Late Species Group on large supports. See page 95.

If the Shrub Rose is in bloom, an attempt at matching the colours of roses and clematis can be made.

USING THE CLEMATIS

It is often said that clematis should be planted on the shaded side of the object it is meant to cover. The theory is that the sun will draw the plant in the right direction. Unfortunately, you may find there is so much shade that the clematis makes poor growth. In these circumstances it is best to grow the clematis at the side of the shrub and guide it where you want it to go.

Having decided to use a shrub as a support for clematis, it may be possible over a few years, by thoughtful pruning, to make the rose into an ideal rounded support.

The clematis is led to the shrub by the use of green twine or green wire. A meat skewer, placed in the ground near the clematis, can be the starting point and the twine or wire is guided on to the rose and over to a skewer on the opposite side. Several supports can be used to criss-cross the shrub (see Figure 18). A cane can be used for the same purpose but removed when the clematis is firmly on the shrub; canes tend to be unsightly.

The number of clematis for each shrub is judged by the size of the shrub and the vigour of the clematis. The number can range from two to six or more.

The clematis can be mixed or all the same. The latter gives a dramatic effect.

It is possible to have a sequence of flowering - especially on early flowering Old Shrub Roses such as 'Canary Bird'. There can be a sequence of a mid season Large Flowered Clematis such as 'Hagley Hybrid', a late season flowerer, like 'Gipsy Queen' and a very late flowerer, for instance 'Lady Betty Balfour'.

The clematis can be allowed to mingle with one another, or kept apart.

The colour can be the same for all clematis if required, for example, all white or all red, or it can be a group of clematis of mixed colours.

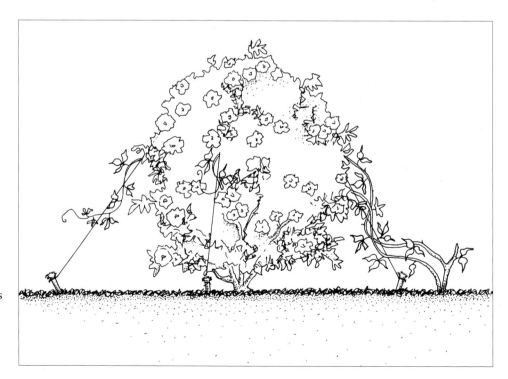

Figure 18. The Clematis is planted 2-3ft. away from the Shrub Rose and discreetly guided towards it by use of green wire or twine.

PLATE 89. This Shrub Rose has completed its flowering and now needs the colour that the Clematis can produce.

With Modern Shrub Roses that repeat flower, matching of the colour of shrub and clematis is described in the principles already discussed.

When the foliage of a shrub is unusual, this gives an opportunity for an exceptional effect. For example, *Rosa glauca* has rather small but brightly coloured pink flowers that are soon gone; they can be replaced with the attractive large bright pink continuously blooming 'Margot Koster' or again 'Margaret Hunt'. Both of these will stand out against the dark foliage.

The clematis planted between the shrubs will often need support in the way of a pillar, a pyramid, an umbrella, a waterfall or cascade frame (see Chapter 12).

Most of the clematis used in the arrangements will be late flowering and therefore needing severe pruning. This can be done in two stages.

In Stage 1, in the autumn, the growth is cut out to a height of 3ft. (91cm.). Gentle tugging will ensure that the growth on the shrub will come away and can be burnt. The remaining stems are brought together with a tie and hidden at the edge of the shrub.

In Stage 2, in the spring, the clematis is finally pruned close to the ground.

PLATE 90. The English rose 'Gertrude Jekyll' is a perfect foil for the single blooms of clematis 'Proteus' at its late summer blooming.

PLATE 91. The Shrub *Rosa rugosa* 'Scabrosa' gives colour and sometimes accompanying hips through a long season. White clematis would be a perfect balance.

PLATE 92. The modern Shrub Rose 'Chinatown' blends well with the Herbaceous *Clematis* × *durandii*.

SUGGESTED COMBINATIONS

Macropetala on supports between unflowering shrubs
C. alpina 'Frances Rivis' flowering on and with 'Canary Bird'
'Lasurstern' on 'Frühlingsmorgen' when it flowers
C. montanas 'Freda' and 'Tetrarose' on pillars alongside 'Nevada'
C. × *durandii* or 'Arabella' over 'Canary Bird' after it flowers
'Margot Koster' over *Rosa glauca*
C. orientalis 'Helios' over 'Ballerina' or 'Graham Thomas' after they flower
'Twilight' with 'Felicia' in flower in late summer
The Viticellas over large Shrubs after they flower
      e.g. 'Penelope', 'Fantin-Latour', 'Frühlingsgold', 'Roseraie de l'Hay'
C. texensis 'Etoile Rose' over 'Buff Beauty' in late summer
C. texensis 'Princess of Wales' over 'Fred Loads' in late summer
C. fargesii 'Flammula', and 'Triternata Rubro-marginata' on supports between Shrub Roses in the autumn

CHAPTER NINE

Clematis With Bedding Roses

Clematis are not only climbers but also clamberers and sprawlers. Herein lies an opportunity to use them with Bedding Roses. Rose beds can line walls, paths and hedges and serve as flanking beds. They can also be isolated in a lawn as island beds which can be round, oval, square or rectangular (see Figure 22). A curve is always more attractive than a straight edge. Again, Bedding Roses are increasingly being planted as groups in herbaceous borders.

Hybrid Tea Roses and Floribunda Roses can be mixed. Plant the taller varieties at the back of your flanking border or at the centre of your island borders. A bed can be planted with one well-chosen variety for the best effect. Another method is to plant in groups of four to five varieties in the beds. Sometimes beds have to be filled with a mixture of different roses. Height can be given to the beds by adding one or more pillars supporting a Climbing Rose and a clematis.

The term 'bedding' is extended to include not only the Hybrid Teas and Floribundas, normally associated with rose beds and borders, but also the Patio Roses used as edging plants in borders, and the short Shrub Roses used as ground cover plants in beds and borders.

Some Bedding Roses are grown as standards or weeping standards, i.e. there is a long supported stem from the ground. For these use the methods employed for Climbing Roses. Clematis can be used on the Bedding Roses before, during or after flowering.

THE ROSES

Roses that can be considered are:
1. Hybrid Tea and Floribunda Roses in beds and borders
2. Patio Roses as edging plants in borders
3. Ground Cover Shrub Roses in beds and borders. This use is likely to be particularly rewarding and exciting

Hybrid Teas and Floribunda Roses

Hundreds are available. In such an event we must turn to the tables published under the authority of the Royal National Rose Society. The top six Hybrid Teas (HT) are taken with the top six Floribundas (cluster-flowerers) (FL). In the latter group I have added a particular proven favourite - 'Pink Parfait'. The roses are listed in alphabetical order:

'Elina' HT - Ivory with lemon centre. Vigorous. Fragrant. Lovely, tall foliage.

'Fragrant Cloud' HT - Geranium-red. Very fragrant. Glossy foliage. A fine bedder.

'Iceberg' FL - Pure white. Vigorous. Tall bush.

'Just Joey' HT - Coppery-orange. Ruffled petals. Bushy. Fragrant. Popular. Winner of International Competition, New Zealand, November 1994.

'Korresia' FL - Yellow. Double blooms. Fragrant. Medium bush.

'Margaret Merril' FL - Pearly-white. Very vigorous. Fragrant. Medium bush.

'Peace' HT - Pale yellow, edged pink. Slight fragrance. Large plant. Still a great favourite.

'Pink Parfait' FL - Shades of pink and cream. No fragrance. Vigorous. Medium bush.

'Savoy Hotel' HT - Light pink. Large double blooms. Some fragrance. Fine foliage.

'Sexy Rexy' FL - Rose pink. Vigorous. Light fragrance. Medium bush.

'Silver Jubilee' HT - Salmon pink. Vigorous. Fragrant. Very popular. Excellent habit.

'Trumpeter' FL - Bright red. Slight fragrance. Short bush.

Selection

> If only one plant - 'Pink Parfait'
>
> If only three plants - 'Pink Parfait', 'Peace', 'Just Joey'

Patio Roses (Dwarf Floribundas)

Developed in recent years these are scaled down Floribundas with clusters of flowers. Useful for edges of borders or beds.

'Anna Ford' - Deep orange with yellow eye. Glossy foliage. Slight fragrance.

'Cider Cup' - Apricot-pink blooms in clusters. Very vigorous. Slight fragrance.

'Gentle Touch' - Pale pink. Clusters of double blooms. Light perfume. Small bush.

'Queen Mother' - Pink. Semi-double blooms. Light fragrance. Vigorous.

'Sweet Dream' - Peachy-apricot. Blooms quartered. Light fragrance. Vigorous. Small bush.

'Sweet Magic' - Deep orange and gold. Good fragrance. Vigorous.

Selection

> If one required - 'Sweet Dream'
>
> If three required - 'Sweet Dream', 'Cider Cup', 'Anna Ford'

Ground Cover Roses

These short roses have been developed to fulfil a need to be trouble free, spreading, weed suppressing and long flowering.

'Essex' - Reddish-pink bloom with white centre. Small starry blooms. No scent. Creeping plant.

'Flower Carpet' - Deep pink with white centres. Semi-double blooms. Slight fragrance. Very vigorous. Medium-sized plant. Disease resistant. A new star.

'Grouse' - Blush-white with yellow stamens. Very vigorous. Spreading large plant to 10ft. (3m.). No scent.

'Kent' - White. Semi-double blooms. Slight fragrance. Small hips in autumn. 18in. (45cm.) by 3ft. (91cm.).

'Nozomi' - Blush-pink and white. Clusters of small starry blooms. Slight fragrance. A proven favourite. Medium-sized plant.

'Suma' - Seedling of 'Nozomi'. Red and pink. Small double blooms. Medium spreading plant to 5ft. (1.5m.).

'White Flower Carpet' - White. Clusters of semi-double blooms. Vigorous. Some scent. Large plant.

Selection

> If one plant to be grown - 'Flower Carpet'
>
> If three plants to be grown - 'Flower Carpet', 'Grouse', 'Nozomi'.

PLATE 93. A mixed bed of roses.

PLATE 94. A typical Hybrid Tea Bedding Rose with single large blooms.

PLATE 95. The cluster head of the Floribunda 'Pink Parfait'.

PLATE 96. The popular Ground Cover Rose 'Nozomi'.

PLATE 97. Clematis 'General Sikorski' makes a perfect match with this glorious yellow English Rose 'Graham Thomas'.

THE CLEMATIS

If we consider each group of Small Flowered Clematis in turn it will become apparent what use can be made of each one.

Clematis from the Evergreen Group have no use as they are too vigorous and would swamp these low growing roses.

The Alpina and Macropetala Groups flower early, could use the Bedding Roses for temporary support but cannot be pruned off the roses. They can, however, be pulled aside so as not to hamper the flowering and growth of the roses.

The Montana Group is too swamping to be used with Bedding Roses.

The Rockery Clematis flower early and could be used between low growing Bedding Roses to give colour before the roses are in bloom.

The Herbaceous Clematis flower late and could either match flowering on the roses or give colour after the roses bloom. By their habit they are more suitable in borders than in beds.

The Viticella Group can flower with the Bedding or Border Roses or can give colour after the roses bloom. An excellent group for our purpose.

The Texensis Group can flower with the Bedding and Border Roses or can give colour after the roses bloom.

The Orientalis Group are too vigorous for these roses with the exception of 'Helios' which could be used to flower with the roses or give colour after the roses flower.

The Late Species Group are too vigorous to use with these roses.

The Early Large Flowered Clematis have one great disadvantage that makes them of limited value. As the clematis are lightly pruned the bulk of the plant remains on the bed or border and is unsightly for most of the year.

The Late Large Flowered Clematis are of special value. After they have bloomed they can have an immediate pruning to reduce them to 3ft. (91cm.). Tied together they can be slipped between the roses and are unobtrusive.

CLEMATIS BEFORE THE BEDDING ROSES FLOWER

Figure 19. Early flowering clematis can meander over roses before the roses flower

The roses are Hybrid Teas and Floribundas in beds, Ground Cover Roses in beds, Patio Roses on border edges, or Hybrid Teas and Floribunda Roses in borders.

The Alpina and Macropetala Groups (p.19) flower before the roses. The roses can be used as supports for the clematis on the edge of beds or in borders, thus giving the clematis height. It would be undesirable to have the clematis on the roses after the former flower as they would mar the flowering of the roses. Thus they should be brought forward after flowering to fall over the path or low wall.

The Rockery Group (p.21) can give colour to a rose bed before the roses flower. They tend to be delicate and would be best grown in pots and planted between Ground Cover Roses. After flowering the pots can remain in the ground until the winter and then be protected in a greenhouse.

Suggested Combinations
    'Macropetala' supported by 'Iceberg'
    C. alpina 'Frances Rivis' supported by 'Peace'
    Plants of *C.* x *cartmanii* 'Joe' between plants of 'Nozomi'

CLEMATIS WHEN THE BEDDING ROSES FLOWER

Figure 20. Clematis can meander over roses in flower with an opportunity to match the colour of the flowers

Here there is a great opportunity for matching the blooms of the clematis and the roses on the principles discussed earlier (see Plates 97 and 98).

Maximum impact is obtained if a number of the same roses are used with a number of the same clematis. This also allows for more accurate matching, for example, a number of 'Perle d'Azur' with a number of 'Peace'.

To be sure the blooming of clematis and roses coincides, a sequence of clematis

115

can be used such as, 'Hagley Hybrid' (pink) followed by *C. viticella* 'Mme Julia Correvon' (red) and followed by 'Ville de Lyon' (wine-red) - on a bed of roses.

The groups of clematis that can be used are Viticellas (p.22), Texensis (p.23) and Late Large Flowered Clematis (p.24). *C. orientalis* 'Helios is best used in a border. The same applies to the Herbaceous Clematis. Of these the Integrifolia section (p.22) including 'Arabella' and *C.* x *durandii*, are especially suitable.

Suggested Combinations
 C. viticella 'Etoile Violette' on a bed of 'Just Joey'
 'Perle d'Azur' on a bed of 'Sweet Dream'
 'Gipsy Queen' on a bed of 'Anna Ford'
 C. orientalis 'Helios' on 'Flower Carpet'
 C. viticella 'Royal Velours' on 'Nozomi'
 C. texensis 'Gravetye Beauty' on a bed of 'Grouse'
 'Prince Charles' on a bed of 'Peace'

CLEMATIS AFTER THE BEDDING ROSES FLOWER

Figure 21. After the roses flower they can be used for support by flowering clematis

By early autumn most of the Bedding Roses will be out of flower or the main blush will be over. Some clematis will still be in flower and can be used to give colour to the Bedding Roses either in a bed, a border or the edging of borders.

Suitable late flowering clematis are: the Late Large Flowering Clematis (p.24), especially very late flowerers such as 'Ville de Lyon', 'Huldine', 'Lady Betty Balfour', 'Madame Baron Veillard', the Viticella group (p.22), the Herbaceous Group (p.22), and the Texensis Group (p.23).

No matching of flowers is required here. The roses act as support for the clematis and the latter provide colour.

As will be mentioned later, the clematis, after flowering, can be pruned off the roses.

Suitable combinations
 'Huldine' on a bed of 'Grouse'
 'Ville de Lyon' on a bed of 'Suma'
 'Lady Betty Balfour' on a bed of 'Silver Jubilee'
 C. viticella 'Blue Belle' on a bed of 'Flower Carpet'
 C. texensis 'Sir Trevor Lawrence' on a bed of 'Essex'
 C. integrifolia 'Rosea' on a bed of 'Nozomi'

PLATE 98. Viticella 'Royal Velours' shows up well against the blooms of rose 'Nozomi'.

PLATE 99. 'Gipsy Queen' on a bed of roses after the roses have flowered.

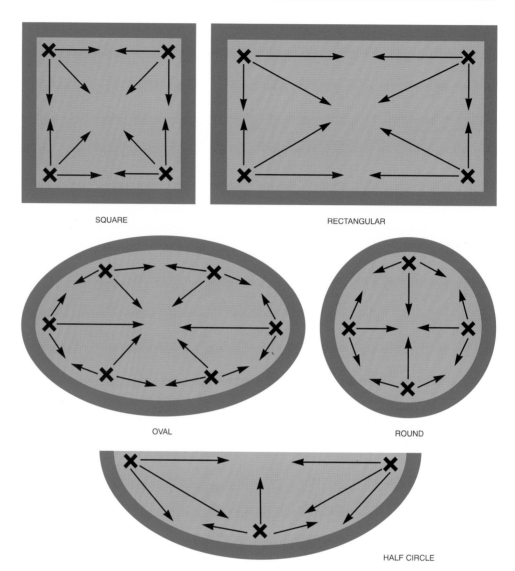

SQUARE

RECTANGULAR

OVAL

ROUND

HALF CIRCLE

Figure 22. Shapes of beds vary. Clematis can be placed at **x** as suggested below. The number of clematis will depend on the size of the bed

USING THE CLEMATIS

The clematis will be employed on roses in three positions – in beds, in borders, on edges of borders.

The size of bed will determine the number of roses planted in it. In turn the number of roses will determine the number of clematis necessary to cover the bed. The clematis must not swamp the roses. Again the vigour of the clematis will dictate the number of plants to be used. For example, 'Perle d'Azur', because of its vigour, will cover twice the area of 'Hagley Hybrid'.

The clematis can be planted at points on the periphery of the bed - square, oblong, oval, round (see Figure 22).

As in many artistic efforts, round shapes tend to be more attractive than straight-sided.

To be effective, and not to swamp the roses, the clematis may need some discreet guidance and training. The gardener must determine the direction he wants each stem to go and to achieve this he sticks in a few thin green canes (as used for potting). These can be pushed in or pulled out to reach the height of the roses and thus remain unobtrusive. As the stem of the clematis extends, it is tied to the cane on the

Figure 23. Clematis can be guided the way you want them to go by tying their stems to green canes placed in a line

plant's intended path. The clematis can be guided straight over the rose or alongside it as required. A perfectionist may choose to connect the canes with string or wire.

The roses may be of a single variety and colour (the best method) or a combination of varieties.

The clematis may be of a single variety and colour (the best method) or there may be a number of different colours.

The number of roses in a border will, again, vary from a group containing few to a long sweep. Sufficient clematis will be used to service a given number of roses, and, once again, the clematis will be discreetly guided towards the gardener's elected path by the use of training.

Patio Roses on the edge of borders can again, of course, vary in number with a sufficient number of clematis used to service them. Again, discreet training will be required.

To encourage the Ground Cover Roses to cover their allotted space, the rose stems can be pegged with bent wire to the ground.

The clematis mentioned above, with the exception of the Alpina, Macropetala and Rockery Groups, can be pruned down to 2-3ft. (60-90cm.) after flowering to tidy the beds. The stems can be discreetly tied together and hidden amongst the roses. They can be pruned almost to ground level in early spring as this pruning not only tidies the bed but allows the spring bulbs to be seen amongst the roses.

SUGGESTED COMBINATIONS

If a bed of roses is of a predominant colour, it is possible to recommend clematis that will blend with those colours:

Yellow rose beds - Clematis 'Perle d'Azur', 'Prince Charles', 'Victoria' and many of the blue/mauve clematis.

White rose beds - *Clematis viticella* 'Margot Koster', 'Margaret Hunt', *C. viticella* 'Mme Julia Correvon', *C. viticella* 'Minuet' and most of the pink/red Late Large Flowered Clematis.

Red rose beds - 'Huldine', *C. viticella* 'Alba Luxurians', *C. viticella* 'Little Nell' and most of the white Late Large Flowered Clematis.

Orange rose beds - *C. viticella* 'Venosa violacea', *C. viticella* 'Etoile Violette', 'Gipsy Queen' and most of the mauve/purple Late Large Flowered Clematis.

PLATE 100. The delicate beauty of the clematis 'Dawn' appears in early season in the flora of the patio.

Figure 24. Clematis can be planted in separate containers from the rose

CHAPTER TEN
Roses and Clematis together in Containers

PRINCIPLES

The rose and clematis can be planted in the same large container (see Figure 25). Another way is to place the clematis in separate containers and move them to the rose when ready to flower (see Figure 24). In this way a succession of clematis can be supplied from a nursery plot.

We are in an era of smaller, labour saving gardens with much more stone and ornaments used in restricted areas. Containers with flowers are required to colour areas – such as patios, terraces, roof gardens, porches, paved paths, stone steps, pillars, columns and arches.

We have to remind ourselves that container, tub or pot plants will not be in mother earth and therefore are completely dependent on the grower.

There has to be care in the selection of the size of container because they quite often have to be moved. Size will depend not only on the strength of the gardener but whether or not additional help is available. A wheeled platform can be purchased for moving containers (see Figure 26).

Container plants are very dependent on an adequate and continual supply of water but must not be over-watered. The containers must be near a water source, not least because watering can be a demanding job.

In planting we need to remember the plants will require nourishment, light, water and oxygen for the roots. Those who have a conservatory, garden room or well lit entrance hall can also have the containers in these places as roses and clematis will flower earlier indoors. If a corner of the garden can be put aside for a nursery bed then the containers can be moved in and out of the indoor situation according to the season. If the plants show signs of distress they can recover within two to three days if placed outside and brought in again.

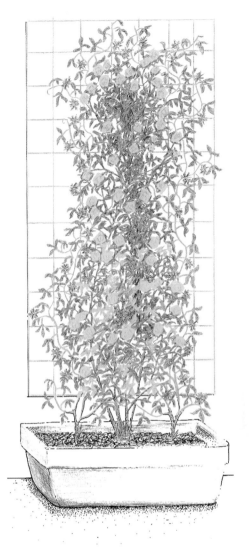

Figure 25. Clematis can be planted in the same container as the rose

ADVANTAGES OF CONTAINERS

Where there is no garden, as on the balcony of an apartment, containers come into their own. When space is limited, as often happens in patio areas in the modern garden, again, containers can be very useful.

In very cold areas clematis and roses grown in containers can be moved to shelter in the winter.

Figure 26. This wheeled plant trolley will help to move heavy containers

DISADVANTAGES OF CONTAINER GROWING

The season in containers is shorter than in the garden.
The blooms in a container plant tend to be smaller.
The plant in the container needs to be repotted every three to five years.
The container will need watering at least daily in the growing season and it may be twice a day in very hot weather.
Plants in containers need more care than when planted in the ground.

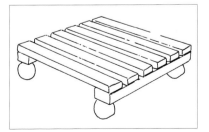

Figure 27. Containers come in many varieties

TYPES OF CONTAINERS

Containers can be round, square or oblong and materials can be stone, soft porcelain, earthenware, metal, fibreglass, wood or plastic (see Figure 27). Stone containers are best for retaining moisture and insulating the plant while terracotta pots can be attractive but it is important to be sure they are frost resistant. 'Thrown' pots are resistant but 'cast' pots (line visible) are not. Concrete pots are very heavy and best avoided unless no other material is available.

Half-barrel wood containers are suitable. All wooden containers should be treated with a safe preservative.

A container should hold a minimum of 4-8 gallons (12-30 litres) of planting medium. It is important to have adequate depth in the container - 18in. (46cm.) minimum. The minimum diameter should be 12in. (30.5cm.) for a single plant.

SELECTION OF ROSES AND CLEMATIS

Both the roses and the clematis should, if possible, have a long flowering period. At the same time both plants should be compact as they are in a confined area. The best rose companions for clematis are the Climbing Roses. The Modern Shrub Rose, if it is repeat flowering, can also be considered. Miniature Climbing Roses are a most promising development.

Two to three clematis can be employed for each rose and it is advantageous if the three are of the same pruning type. In addition to the shorter Large Flowered Hybrids, the Viticellas, the Alpinas and Macropetalas can make useful companions to the roses.

The clematis can all be the same variety or mixed and can flower together or in sequence. They can all be the same colour or have different colours.

PLANTING IN THE CONTAINER

The single most important aspect of planting is to make sure that there is adequate drainage. If the roots continually lie in a pool of water they will lack oxygen and the plant will not flourish.

Check carefully that there are adequate drainage holes in the base of the container. It may be advantageous to increase the number of holes to guarantee good drainage. Broken pottery or stones should be put over the holes for easy drainage. An insecticide can be sprayed into this and the planting material then placed above. The container must be held off the ground by tiles or stones - again to encourage drainage (see Figure 28).

Gardeners have their favourite material for containers. The famous gardener Ernest Markham used three parts loam to one part leaf mould. To this he added wood ash and bonemeal. Some coarse sand was added to assist drainage. Another formula would be two parts soil, one part compost, one part grit and to this is added slow release fertiliser or bonemeal. If in doubt use John Innes No 3 - three parts to

PLATE 101. 'H.F. Young' flowers early in a container and is the best true blue colour of all clematis.

PLATE 102. 'Pink Fantasy' blooms for a long period in mid season as a perfect container plant.

one part grit plus slow release fertiliser. Each spring, one or more handfuls of sulphate of potash (depending on the size of the container) should be worked into the planting material and this should be repeated in midsummer. A 1½in. (4cm.) deep saucer should be left at the top of the container for ease of watering (see Figure 28). A mulch of grit or pebbles should be placed in this to prevent surface growth.

The rose should be planted as in the garden. The rose roots can be pruned to fit the pot. The clematis, as in the garden, should be planted with its crown 3in. (8cm.) below the surface.

In its first year a clematis is usually planted in a 3in. (8cm.) pot. In the second year it is usually moved to a 6in. (15cm.) pot. In the third year it is planted in a

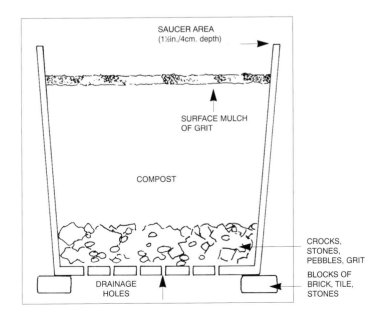

Figure 28. Planting a container

PLATE 103. 'The Vagabond', a clematis for late season, has just been introduced and will make a popular container plant for its vigour yet small size.

12in. (30cm.) pot; mature clematis from this stage are the best for use in containers. Recent research suggests that clematis will make the best progress if planted straight into a 12in. (30cm.) pot.

Both rose and clematis should be hard pruned the first year so as to encourage good growth from the base.

Every year in the spring the top 2-3in. (5-8cm.) of the planting material should be gently removed and replaced with new compost containing bonemeal or slow release fertiliser. Every five years replace all the compost.

Pots of bulbs, geraniums and annuals can be placed on top of the soil in the container but these should never be planted in the soil itself.

If unusually hot, a small container can be insulated and kept moist by putting it in a larger container with moist peat between the two.

TRAINING

The rose should be trained on the wall in the usual fashion or be encouraged to twirl around a pillar. The clematis is then trained on the rose and, if there is room, the clematis can twirl around it like a helix.

WATERING

In the growing season the container must be watered at least once a day. In hot weather this may need to be twice a day. A soluble fertiliser should be supplied with the water and foliar feeding can be useful.

Watering is an easier operation if a saucer area is left at the lip of the container. Experience soon shows how much water is necessary to percolate to the base of the container with this amount then regularly placed in the saucer area. If the container is outside, allowance has to be made for rain.

During the flowering period the soluble potash-based fertiliser should not be applied as it will shorten the flowering period.

In winter the planting material must be moist without being wet.

Signs of underwatering are: the soil is dry when felt 2in. (5cm.) below the surface. Young shoots droop. Leaves are pointed downwards.

Signs of overwatering are: falling leaves, yellow leaves at base of the plants.

PLATE 104. The rose 'Casino' is one of the best yellows to lighten a patio.

CONTAINER POSITION

It is best to avoid having the container facing south as the heat will call for more watering although this will, of course, sometimes be unavoidable.

WIND DAMAGE

The roses should be tied firmly to their support and the clematis tied firmly to the rose.

Figure 29. A container can be wrapped in a layer of bubble polythene and an outer layer of hessian or netting

PRUNING

Whatever the variety, clematis should be severely pruned the first year to encourage strong growth from the base. The roses can be pruned after flowering in the summer or left until the spring. Judicious pruning of the rose can improve its value as a support for the clematis.

WINTER CARE OF CONTAINERS

Compost in the containers can freeze solid during cold spells and plants can suffer root death and dehydration. Repeat thawing and freezing is particularly damaging. Consequently the containers should be protected by wrapping them in bubble polythene, sacking, or a coat made of bin liners stuffed with paper, straw, leaves or similar materials (see Figure 29).

If the containers are movable they should be placed in a sheltered spot during very cold weather, or, if mobile, they can be buried up to their necks in a trench. Insulating material such as leaves, bracken or conifer branches can them be placed over them. In exceptionally cold weather the containers should be moved indoors, into a shed, garage or greenhouse but care must be exercised not to let them dry out.

PLATE 105. The rose 'Danse Du Feu' has been a favourite for a long time, appeals for its rich scarlet colour and can be used in a container.

SELECTED CLEMATIS FOR PLANTING WITH ROSES

Very early season
The Alpina Group - variety of colours (pp.59-60)
The Macropetala Group - variety of colours (pp.60-61)

Early season
The Early Large Flowered Group:
'Alice Fisk' (wisteria blue)
'Anna' (pink)
'Arctic Queen' (double white)
'Barbara Jackman' (striped)
'Dawn' (pink and white)
'Edith' (white)
'Fair Rosamond' (white)
'Fireworks' (striped)
'Guernsey Cream' (creamy-yellow)
'H. F. Young' (blue)
'Lasurstern' (deep mauve)
'Miss Bateman' (white)
'Nelly Moser' (striped)
'Sealand Gem' (lavender blue)

Mid season
'John Warren' (pink)
'Mrs Cholmondeley' (blue)
'Multi-blue' (double blue)

'Proteus' (light mauve double)
'Richard Pennell' (purple)
'Royal Velvet' (red-purple)
'The President' (dark blue)
'Snow Queen' (white)

Late season
The Viticella Group:
'Abundance' (red)
'Etoile Violette' (dark blue)
'Madame Julia Correvon' (red and white)
'Venosa Violacea' (white and blue)
'Royal Velours' (velvety-red)
The Late Large Flowered Group:
'Allanah' (red)
'Comtesse de Bouchaud' (pink)
'Hagley Hybrid' (pink)
'John Huxtable' (white)
'Pink Fantasy' (pink)
'Prince Charles' (light blue)
'Niobe' (red)
'The Vagabond'
'Twilight' (blue)

Very late season
'Lady Betty Balfour' (blue)

PLATE 106. The tendency of the rose 'Summer Wine' to change its glorious colour almost every day must make it a talking point on a patio.

SELECTED ROSES FOR CONTAINERS

'Bantry Bay' (rose pink)
'Casino' (yellow)   (see Plate 104)
'Danse du Feu' (red)   (see Plate 105)
'Galway Bay' (glowing pink)(see Plate 43)
'Golden Showers' (yellow)   (see Plate 59)
'Handel' (pink and white)   (see Plates 61, 113)
'New Dawn' (white)   (see Plates 20, 55, 58, 118, 121)
'Parkdirektor Riggers' (red) (see Plate 67)
'Pink Perpétue' (deep pink) (see Plates 42, 46, 123, 131)
'Schoolgirl' (orange)   (see Plates 60, 77)
'Swan Lake' (white)
'Warm Welcome' (orange)

SUGGESTED COMBINATIONS

Macropetala on any of the above roses before they flower
'Dawn' and 'Miss Bateman' with 'Danse du Feu'
'Victoria' and 'Gipsy Queen' with 'Casino'
'H. F. Young' or 'Lasurstern' with 'Golden Showers'
'Hagley Hybrid' and 'Comtesse de Bouchaud' with 'Parkdirektor Riggers'
'Allanah' with 'Swan Lake'
'Prince Charles' with 'Golden Showers'
'Barbara Jackman' or 'H. F. Young' or 'Lasurstern' with 'New Dawn'
'Mrs Cholmondeley' with 'Golden Showers' or 'Schoolgirl'
'Prince Charles' with 'New Dawn'
'Lady Betty Balfour' with 'New Dawn'
'Gipsy Queen' or 'Victoria' or *C. viticella* 'Etoile Violette' with 'Pink Perpétue'

PLATE 107. Rose 'Pink Parfait' and clematis 'Victoria' are combined to produce a stunning display.

PLATE 108. An arrangement using the beautiful rose 'Casino' with clematis 'Blue Belle' and 'Lady Betty Balfour' produces a striking display of blooms and seed heads.

CHAPTER ELEVEN
Roses and Clematis as Cut Flowers

The pleasure of combining roses and clematis need not be restricted to the garden as they can be brought indoors and combined as cut flowers.

AVAILABLE MATERIAL

Roses
In the case of roses the season starts with the early Shrub Roses and reaches its peak with the main crop in early and midsummer. Some roses will produce sporadic but worthy blooms into early winter.

The Floribundas produce clusters of colourful bloom while the Hybrid Teas and Climbing Hybrid Teas produce large, eye-catching blooms.

PLATE 109. A small but effective arrangement combining rose 'Iceberg' and clematis 'Star of India'.

The roses listed below can produce sprays for cutting
(To match the many blue/mauve clematis a number of apricot/yellow/orange roses are included here)

'Canary Bird' (Shrub) - yellow
'Casino' (Climber) - yellow
'Cider Cup' (Patio Rose) - pink
'Cornelia' (Shrub) - pink
'Felicia' (Shrub) - pink
'Fred Loads' (Shrub) - red
'Gentle Touch' (Patio Rose) - pink
'Golden Showers' (Climbing) - yellow
'Iceberg' (FL) - white
'Nevada' (Shrub) - white
'Pink Perpétue' (Climber) - deep pink
'Schoolgirl' (Climber) - apricot

The roses listed below can produce single blooms for cutting:
All are Hybrid Teas unless otherwise indicated.
(To exploit the blue/mauve clematis a number of apricot/yellow/orange roses are included in this list)

'Anne Harkness' (FL) - yellow
'Apricot Silk' - apricot
'Belle Blonde' - golden-yellow
'Bettina' - orange
'Buff Beauty' (Shrub) - yellow
'Chinatown' (Shrub) - yellow
'Diorama' - yellow
'Elina' - white
'Fragrant Cloud' - red
'Freedom' - deep yellow
'Geraldine' (FL) - orange
'Gold Star' - deep yellow
'Graham Thomas' (English Rose) - yellow
'Grandpa Dickson' - pale yellow
'Just Joey' - coppery-orange
'Korresia' (FL) - yellow
'Miss Harp' - deep yellow
'Mojave' - orange
'Mountbatten' - yellow
'Peace' - yellow
'Perle d'Or' (Shrub) - apricot
'Pink Parfait' (FL) - pink and cream
'Remember Me' - orange
'Savoy Hotel' - light pink
'Sexy Rexy' (FL) - rose-pink
'Simba' - yellow
'Southampton' (FL) - apricot-orange

About a third of the stem with the bloom should be taken and the stem cut, if possible, above an outward facing bud. In general the harder the rose is pruned the larger, but fewer, roses it will produce. If a major interest is roses for the house there may be advantages in having a bed of roses cultivated for this purpose. Rich fertilising will produce good blooms. Rose foliage can make an interesting partner to clematis. Furthermore, rose hips in the autumn can be used for matching either clematis blooms or clematis seed heads.

Clematis

Flowers appear earlier in the clematis than in the rose. As early as midwinter the blooms of *C. cirrhosa* are available for cutting in long strands - up to 3½ft. (1m.) long. In late winter the lovely *C. armandii* produces an abundance of sweetly scented white and pink blooms which again can be in 3½ft. (1m.) strands. Then come the delicate bells of the Alpinas and the double bells of the Macropetalas. The clematis we have mentioned will all have to be displayed on their own as no roses will be available unless grown under glass or imported from favourable climates. Rose foliage, when suitable, can be used in combination.

The roses soon appear, however, and are available for matching with perhaps the most spectacular companion being the Large Flowered Clematis. In general the most useful are those with long firm stems such as early favourites like white 'Henryi', the dramatic 'Miss Bateman', the colourful striped 'Barbara Jackman' and 'Fireworks', the purple 'The President' and blue 'Lasurstern'. Later come 'Kathleen Wheeler', 'Lawsoniana' and 'W. E. Gladstone'. Later still are found the Jackmanii Group including 'Comtesse de Bouchaud', 'Gipsy Queen', 'Hagley Hybrid', 'Jackmanii', 'Perle d'Azur' and 'Victoria'. Very late, 'Huldine' is noted for its striking semi-translucent white flower. Multiples such as the early 'Beauty of Worcester' and the elegant 'Vyvyan Pennell' should not be overlooked. To produce good flowers for cutting Large Flowered Clematis should have harder pruning than is usual.

To coincide with the rose harvest are notable contributors from the Small Flowered Clematis. Of exceptional worthiness is 'Integrifolia Durandii', one of the Herbaceous Clematis. Other Integrifolias are meritorious especially 'Rosea' and 'Arabella'. Of the Heracleifolias, 'Edward Prichard' stands out for its fragrance, long purple buds, and attractive purple and white flowers hanging in panicles. Herbaceous varieties last well in water. Almost all the Viticellas are good cutting flowers with 'Purpurea Plena Elegans' being a special point of interest with its dark double blooms. Just one tulip-shaped bloom of the Texensis Group can add immediate interest to an arrangement. *C. fusca* may lack beauty but it is so unusual that it shines as a focus of conversation. The Orientalis Group, especially the exceptional 'Bill Mackenzie', brings in the colour yellow. *C. flammula* (white) and *C.* x *triternata* Rubro-marginata (white and pink) used in quantity make a perfect background to roses – and are richly scented. Do not overlook the native clematis such as 'Vitalba' in Europe, 'Virginiana' in the USA and 'Aristata' in Australia as all will give an abundant supply of blooms in late summer.

In Holland and Germany there are now nurseries specialising in producing clematis as cut flowers.

Some roses have attractive hips, some clematis attractive seed heads and the two can be combined.
Roses for hips are:

'Fru Dagmar Hastrup' - large, tomato-like
'Harvest Home' - tomato-like
Rosa davidii - flask-shaped, red
Rosa glauca - round, red
Rosa moyesii 'Geranium' - elongated, scarlet
Rosa roxburghii - prickly
Rosa rugosa Alba - tomato-like, red
Rosa rugosa Scabrosa - large, red
Rosa soulieana - small, orange
Rosa spinosissima - small, black
Rosa virginiana - small, red
'Sealing Wax' - flask-shaped

Clematis for Attractive Seed Heads are:

C. alpina
C. chiisanensis
C. fargesii
C. flammula
C. macropetala
C. napulensis (conservatory plant)
C. orientalis
C. serratifolia
C. tangutica
C. virginiana
C. vitalba

A number of clematis have attractive foliage that can be used as a background for roses when their flowers have gone – *C. cirrhosa* has fine, delicate, fern-like foliage, as does *C. ladakhiana*, while *C. armandii* has green leathery leaves. Some of the Orientalis Group have finely cut foliage.

Again, some roses have foliage that makes an attractive background for clematis, for example, the coppery-mauve leaves of *Rosa glauca*, the light green leaves of *Rosa virginiana*, the fern-like foliage of *Rosa willmottiae* and the grey-green leaves of *Rosa villosa*.

PLATE 110. Colour and shape are features of these seed heads of a macropetala.

PLATE 111. Roses and clematis show an elegant and delicate beauty in this novel water arrangement.

COLLECTING THE FLOWERS

Rose and clematis flowers should be cut in the evening. Discard damaged or spent flowers; earwigs can damage the clematis blooms in the late summer. Discard flowers with weak stems. The flower should not be fully open and on a strong firm stem. Remove some of the leaves, especially with the clematis, to reduce the loss of water through transpiration. The ends of the stems should be crushed and dipped in boiling water or held over a lighted candle for a few seconds. Immediately (this is important) immerse the flowers up to their necks in water and leave overnight. The flower may benefit from a little sugar in the morning.

DISPLAYING THE CLEMATIS

The container should be carefully selected to match and enhance the beauty of that particular flower combination. A large variety of vases or vessels of varying colours in glass or pottery can be employed.

Set the arrangement against a suitable physical background. Thought should be given to natural lighting although artificial lighting can sometimes enhance the arrangement.

The great merit of clematis as a partner is that with an absence of blue in roses it can supply precisely that colour. When only a few flowers of roses and clematis are employed then the use of an interesting piece of wood can add interest.

Just one clematis and one rose can be most effective in a glass container, coloured to suit the combination.

As clematis prefer not to be in oasis, the roses can be in foam (oasis) and the clematis in the water nearby lying free or being supported by florists' cones.

For each pint (½ litre) of water in the plant holder add a teaspoon full of sugar (as a nutrient) and half a teaspoon full of bleach (to kill bacteria). The flowers should last five to ten days. Should the flowers show signs of drooping then 1in. (2.5cm.) should be cut off each stem and the flowers put into water up to their necks overnight.

Top the container up with water as you are dealing with thirsty plants.

An unusual way of displaying both clematis and roses is to float them on water, either in a glass or pottery vessel. The stems are cut to 1in. (2.5cm.) and the flowers are allowed to rest in the bowl of water. The pattern can vary with the selection of roses and clematis. This is a very quick and effective way of making a talking point for a lunch or dinner party.

The clematis seed heads can also be preserved by cutting them while they are still green. The same applies to trailing stems. The stems are placed in a mixture of glycerine and hot water (one part glycerine to two parts hot water). The mixture must be well mixed until it is clear or the glycerine will remain at the bottom. Woody stems can be put into the hot mixture. For soft material such as seed heads allow the mixture to cool. Treatment in the fluid is for seven to fourteen days depending on the thickness of the material.

SUGGESTED COMBINATIONS

R. 'Casino' and C. 'Victoria'
R. 'Mountbatten' and C. 'The President'
R. 'Pink Parfait' and C. 'Etoile Violette'
R. 'Pink Perpétue' and C. 'General Sikorski'
R. 'Iceberg' and C. 'Rouge Cardinal'
R. 'Elina' and C. 'Niobe'
R. 'Just Joey' and C. 'Perle d'Azur'
R. 'Fragrant Cloud' and C. 'Marie Boisselot'
R. 'Galway Bay' and C. 'Huldine'
R. 'Korresia' and C. 'Twilight'
R. 'Nevada' and C. 'Rosea'
R. 'Bettina' and C. 'Integrifolia Durandii'.

CHAPTER TWELVE
Cultivation of Roses and Clematis

TOOLS FOR THE JOB

A Planting Plan

Labels seem to have a life of their own. They come and go. They disappear. Thus it is essential to have a plan of the garden which clearly shows the position of each rose and clematis. This can be part of an already existing garden plan or it can be created just for roses and clematis.

It is useful to divide the garden into sections giving each a name. For example, 'the oval bed', 'the north bed', 'the long bed', etc. Each section can have a page of the plan to itself and a particular mark such as an 'O' can indicate a rose while another mark, such as an 'X', can indicate the position of a clematis. Each mark thus bears a name, rose or clematis.

To make it easy and to recognise instantly the position of a rose or clematis it is useful to mark in on the plan permanent structures such as posts, trees, marks on walls, etc. These permanent structures are named on the plan, with the positions of the roses and clematis shown in relation to them, thus making the latter easy to find.

The plan will be invaluable in the winter when the time comes to plan new plantings for the following year. Indeed, on the plan it is possible to mark further positions for roses or clematis with a broken circle or broken cross.

Cultivation (see Figure 30)

A fork and spade are essential for digging holes for roses and clematis. If they are of steel, though expensive, they add another dimension of pleasure to the gardening. Medium or small size are best as large tools are tiring.

A trowel is necessary for potting. A hoe is required for the control of weeds. Hoeing should not extend closer than 12in. (30cm.) to a rose or clematis; at that point it is best to do hand weeding. When hoeing, an eye should be kept out for any clematis seedlings in the soil. If large enough they can be potted up at once although it is a chance in a hundred that you will have a winner.

Whenever one gardens some untidiness is bound to occur but nothing polishes up the job better than a gentle rake to restore order.

A wheelbarrow is useful for moving materials around the garden, a two-wheeled variety being especially helpful for the handicapped or the elderly.

Plastic pots of varying sizes will be required for any potting work.

Figure 30. Some of the useful tools for a clematarian

PLATE 112. Rose 'Korona' and clematis 'Victoria' share a cottage wall.

Guiding and Tying (see Figure 31)

It may be necessary to improve on nature by gently guiding clematis or roses in a particular direction for a better effect. This can be done by using garden twine, green string (not very permanent, useful for one season), green wire (more permanent but liable to become loose), and canes. Canes are the easiest to use and give the least work. These can be bamboo canes of various lengths or the shorter green canes used in potting.

Clematis need to be tied to roses or supports and roses also need to be tied to supports. The weakest material is raffia. It does not damage the plants but is rather fiddly and only lasts for one season. Garden twine is used by the experts, but can be time-consuming, and even rope may be required for heavier functions. Wire twist ties covered with either paper or plastic are quick ways of tying clematis to supports and can also be used with roses. The paper-covered variety will only last for one season and is therefore best employed with clematis stems that will be pruned away in the autumn or winter. The plastic-covered wire ties can last for several years. Care must be taken not to crush delicate rose or clematis stems with the ties although the gardener quickly becomes adept at using them in a way that does not cause damage.

Watering (see Figure 32)

Both roses and clematis require watering in dry areas. Clematis are particularly fond of water and this can generally be provided in two ways:
1. Spot watering when the watering is concentrated on one particular plant
2. Area watering when the whole area is given a heavy soaking and all the plants in that area receive water.

Figure 31. Means of tying and guiding clematis

PLATE 113. The rose 'Handel' brings light to the beautiful clematis 'Star of India'.

A watering can, which is usually of one gallon (4.5 litres) capacity and constructed of metal or plastic, may be all that is necessary. Of the two materials, plastic is much cheaper. A hose may be used for spot watering. If you water with a hose it is useful to fill the watering can with the hose counting as the filling goes on. You now have a count number for a gallon or 4.5 litres. Now, pointing the hose at the plant and counting, it is possible to gauge the amount of water being given to a plant and to stop when the required amount has been delivered.

A sprinkler will need to be attached to the hose for area watering.

A recent development is the extensive use of a seep hose that leaks water into the beds. This method saves water and is effective but the hose can become clogged and is sold with a substance for unclogging.

Spraying
A compression sprayer is required as insecticides and fungicides may need to be sprayed on roses and clematis.

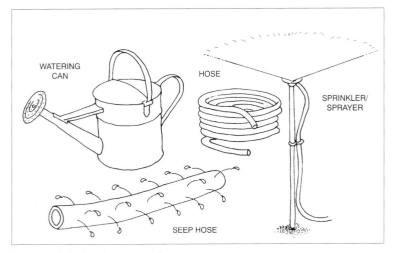

Figure 32. Watering methods

Later it should be mentioned that by employing systemic chemicals the material can be watered into the ground around the plant. A systemic chemical is taken in by the roots and is spread everywhere through the sap of the plants. Putting the material into the ground is not only an effective method but is also safer in that the holder of the sprayer will not inhale the material.

Pruning (see Figure 33)
This is necessary for roses and clematis. As clematis have thinner and weaker stems than roses, much of the pruning can be done with scissors which is both quick and easy. Secateurs will be required for roses and the thicker stems of clematis. With thick rose stems a long handled pruner may be necessary and with really thick stems a pruning saw is both quick and effective.

Chemicals
If possible these should be bought in bulk as they are much cheaper in that form. Although this is already possible with fertilisers, it is still difficult for the amateur gardener to have access to the bulk buying of insecticides and fungicides except perhaps through gardening clubs. All chemicals must be kept in a place of safety away from children and should be used according to the manufacturer's instructions.

Labelling
Labels will be required for roses and clematis and will need to be fixed to the walls, posts, and other supports of the plants. Sometimes they may need to be stuck into the ground in open borders.
This is such an important subject that it will be discussed in detail later (see pages 158-160).

Miscellaneous (see Figure 34)
A boss sheet is useful for placing soil dug out of a hole. It prevents the soil marking the lawn and it is easy, using the sheet, to manoeuvre the soil back into the hole if required.
A kneeling pad assists the gardener when bending down to slip the clematis and roses into the ground. For the elderly a kneeling frame not only makes kneeling easy but also makes rising much easier with the support of the frame.
A measuring rod or ruler makes it possible to measure accurately the width and

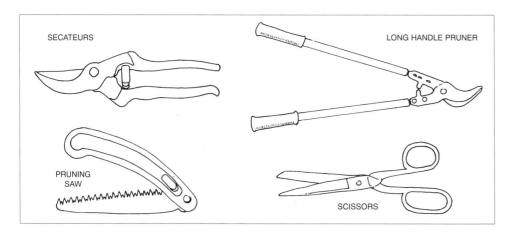

Figure 33. Pruning tools

138

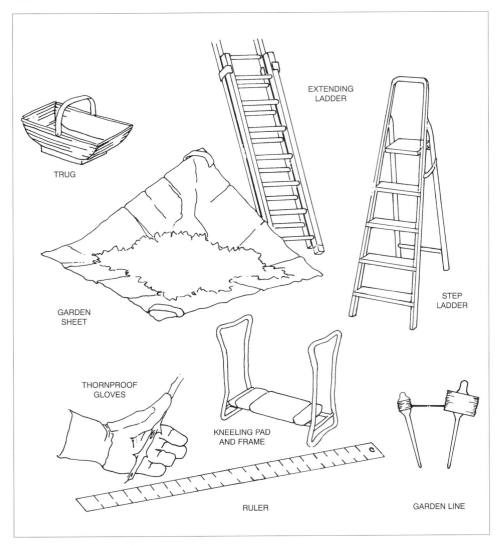

Figure 34.
Miscellaneous gardening
aids

depth of holes and distances between plants. An inexpensive rod can be made out of a 4-6ft. (1-1.5m.) long and 1in. (2.5cm.) square piece of timber on which intervals of 1ft. (30cm.) and then intervals of 3in. (7.5cm.) have been marked.

A garden line is invaluable in creating straight borders.

The best tool of all is the human hand but this is liable to damage. Every worthwhile gardener has occasional bruises and cuts marking successful effort. Honourable wounds! Immunity to tetanus can be guaranteed with a tetanus jab every five years although there are occasions when gloves are essential and one of these is during the pruning of roses.

A trug, expensive in wood but less expensive in plastic, assists the collection of cut flowers.

An aluminium step ladder, 5ft. (1.5m.) long, is light to move around the garden. It will give all the height required for tending the roses and clematis. It can be used with legs apart and safety shelf in operation or with legs closed and leaning on the wall, post, etc. Care must be exercised in the latter event to make sure that the step ladder is secure. Rarely, a rose or clematis may require care at a height from the ground that calls for a ladder. This is one of the most dangerous tasks in the garden and security precautions must be strictly observed.

Lastly, remember that brightly painted tools are easier to find if you mislay them in the garden.

PLATE 114. The clematis 'Comtesse de Bouchaud' is reliable even on a north facing wall. It is seen here climbing into a rose on a pergola at The Garden of the Rose, The Royal National Rose Society, St. Albans, U.K.

PLANTING

The Plan

Plan your planting sometime beforehand. Consult the plan and decide where clematis can be planted with advantage. In the case of spring planting, time can be devoted to the planning during the winter. Indeed, the holes can be prepared during the winter for spring planting. It is said that an hour's gardening in winter is as good as five hours in the summer!

In general the planting of roses and clematis is the same, with a few exceptions. The main planting of roses should be in the autumn. The main planting of clematis should be in the spring. The roots of the rose are more robust than those of clematis and the latter must be treated with care. Roses need planting 1in. (2.5cm.) and clematis 4in. (10cm.) below ground level.

If you have a good, rich, loamy soil then planting is a simple matter. Make a hole deep enough for your rose and clematis and put them in the ground. Most soils, however, need extra humus and nutrients.

PLATE 115. Clematis 'Hagley Hybrid' and rose 'Compassion' produce a cheerful mix of colour.

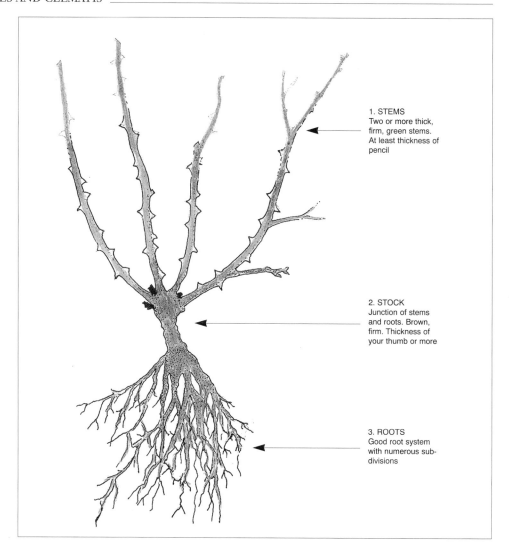

1. STEMS
Two or more thick,
firm, green stems.
At least thickness of
pencil

2. STOCK
Junction of stems
and roots. Brown,
firm. Thickness of
your thumb or more

3. ROOTS
Good root system
with numerous sub-
divisions

Figure 35. Choosing a
rose

Choosing a Plant

When buying a rose or a clematis there is much to be said in favour of buying from
a specialist rose or clematis nursery as here the choice will be wide and expert help
available. Again, the quickest way of gaining access to many roses and clematis and
weighing up their merits is to visit specialist nurseries.

Roses

A Climbing Rose or Shrub should have at least two stems, preferably more, about
30in. (76cm.) long. Even more important is to have a well-developed root system.

Bedding (Bush) Roses should look in good condition and have at least two stems,
preferably more. The area between the stems and the roots, the root stock, should
be thick. The stems should be green and plump, and the wood solid and well-
ripened, and be thicker than a pencil. Again it is vital to have a well-developed root
system. In the autumn, nurseries will supply roses on their bare roots. This is the
cheapest way of buying a rose (see Figure 35).

Container grown roses are available during the growing season and these can be
planted at any time in the year when conditions are favourable. Making sure that
they are continually well-watered is important. Look for a strong growing plant
and check that it has been grown in the container.

Clematis

Clematis plants should be at least two years old. Look for a plant with more than one stem, 2-3ft. (60-90cm.) long. Look for good strong buds low down on the stem. Check that the plant has a good root system by checking the roots are emerging through the drainage holes at the bottom of the pot. If in any doubt, ask the nursery to display the roots to you.

Avoid one year old plants which will be found in 4in. (10cm.) pots and referred in the trade as 'liners'. These are not bred for growing in the ground and if purchased should be repotted into a 2 litre pot and 'grown on' for another year.

Delivery

If you are ordering by post then both rose and clematis will be delivered in the autumn. The roses can be planted at once. There is much to be said for repotting the clematis into a larger pot, keeping it protected and well-watered through the winter and planting it in the spring. It is now becoming more common for clematis nurseries to supply plants ready for planting in the spring. The main reason for nurseries wanting to supply clematis in the autumn is their reluctance to carry them through the winter. However, a container grown clematis can be planted at any time of the year, if conditions are favourable.

Situation

Both roses and clematis grow well in the temperate regions of the world. Ideally both enjoy growing in full sun away from the wind. Both, clematis in particular, object to strong cold winds. When the gardener talks about a sheltered position he means a spot away from cold winds.

Neither rose nor clematis will grow in shade. Both will grow in semi-shade. There are varieties of both that will grow on north facing walls.

Clematis for north facing walls

Alpina Group
'Comtesse de Bouchaud'
C. fargesii
'Hagley Hybrid'
Macropetala Group
'Mrs Cholmondeley'
'Nelly Moser'
'Perle d'Azur'
'Victoria'
Viticella Group

Roses for north facing walls

'Compassion'
'Danse du Feu'
'Maigold'
'Morning Jewel'
'New Dawn'
'Parkdirektor Riggers'
'Pink Perpétue'

PLATE 116. Clematis 'Mrs Cholmondeley' is reliable and continuous blooming even on a north facing wall as seen here.

Both roses and clematis enjoy good drainage. If the site is not well-drained then the roots will be in water. Consequently, if water denies oxygen to the roots, in time the plant will suffer and die.

Soil

The ideal soil is friable, well-drained, and loamy. Given such a soil, planting becomes easy because the soil contains all the necessary conditions for a healthy plant. In practice gardeners do not find themselves with the ideal soil it being either too light or too heavy. If too light then, although the soil is easy to work, water slips through it very easily and it contains little nutriment. Such a soil needs the addition of humus in the form of manure, compost, peat or peat substitutes. A heavy soil may be full of nutriment but lack drainage. Roots require not only water and nutriment but also oxygen. The latter is absent if the roots are continually in water. Care must be taken, therefore, to drain the holes made for planting in a heavy soil and this can be done with broken brick or rubble to a depth of 4-6in. (10-15cm.).

The soil of established rose beds is not a good site for planting new roses. The soil suffers from 'soil sickness' and the new roses do not flourish. This is a big problem in rose growing and the 'sickness' is thought to be due to a fungus. It is advisable to plant the rose in a new bed or to bring in 2ft. (60cm.) or so of fresh soil to the old site.

In the case of clematis it is not thought that old clematis sites develop soil sickness. However, it is known that 'wilt' is less prevalent in fresh soil. Furthermore, clematis are heavy feeders and more likely to exhaust the existing soil. Again, new soil is an advantage in an existing site.

Both roses and clematis grow satisfactorily in soil which is neutral, slightly acid or slightly alkaline. The ideal pH for growing clematis is not yet known as no experimentation has taken place. While the Rockery Clematis are known to like an acid soil, the end result of experimentation is likely to be that clematis will grow well in either slightly alkaline or acid soil.

The hole

In the case of the roses, this should be large enough to take the roots comfortably without them being squeezed together. This is usually in the order of 2ft. (60cm.) wide by 1½ft. (45cm.) deep. Long roots can be trimmed and suckers pulled away. Clematis should have a hole of 18in. (45cm.) diameter and 2ft. (60cm.) deep.

When digging the hole mark out the area on the soil surface. Having removed the top layer with a spade loosen the next layer with a fork before using the spade again to lift the soil out. Keep on loosening the soil with a fork to make your task much easier. Any soil that you discard put in the wheelbarrow and take away. (Keep good topsoil.) The commonest error is not to make the hole wide enough for roses and deep enough for clematis.

When planting, it is convenient to think of five layers in the hole. The first, the bottom layer, is where the roots will be growing. It is known that clematis roots extend for at least 18-24in. (45-60cm.), even 39in. (1m.). Thus about 9in. (23cm.) is given over to this layer, to give roots a good start. The roots need a rich medium for nourishment and one which will retain water. Experts vary in their recommendations – a common one being half soil with half manure or moist, coarse, peat or leaf mould. Another common recommendation is for half soil and

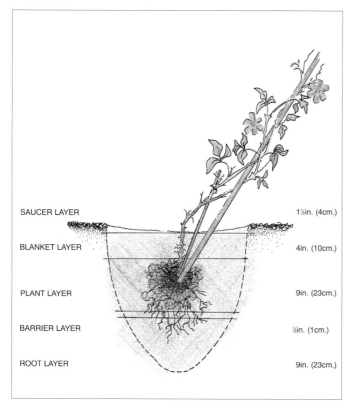

Figure 36. Five layers of planting material in a hole of 1½ft. (45cm.) diameter and 2ft. (60cm.) depth

SAUCER LAYER   1½in. (4cm.)

BLANKET LAYER   4in. (10cm.)

PLANT LAYER   9in. (23cm.)

BARRIER LAYER   ½in. (1cm.)

ROOT LAYER   9in. (23cm.)

half garden compost. Whichever one is employed, two handfuls of bonemeal should also be well mixed in.

The second layer should be a mere ½in. (1cm.) of soil or peat which is simply a barrier to keep the roots of the new plant initially separate from the rich material below.

The third layer of about 9in. (23cm.) is where the rose or clematis will be placed.

The fourth layer is above the clematis or rose and extends to about 4in. (10cm.) as a blanket to the plant. The rose must be planted in this so that its bud union is 1in. (2.5cm.) below the level of the ground. A clematis should be 4in. (10cm.) below ground level. Accuracy can be achieved by a cane crossing the hole from which it can be easily gauged as to where the rose or clematis should lie (see Figure 37).

The material in the third and fourth layers need not be as rich as the material in the bottom area and can consist of good topsoil taken out of the hole or soil mixed with peat, leaf mould or compost. One handful of bonemeal can be added although this should be avoided in light soils as it may attract ants and should be replaced by a general fertiliser.

The fifth layer is the lip area allowing 1in. (4cm.) below the soil level to make a saucer shape into which water can gather either naturally or as the result of watering. Avoid leaving the surface soil convex as a concave surface will greatly facilitate the task of watering (see Figure 36).

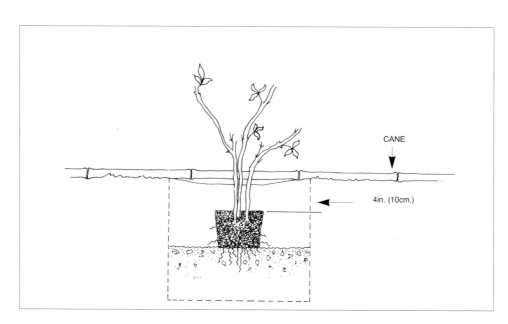

CANE

4in. (10cm.)

Figure 37. Judging depth of planting by using a cane

PLATE 117. The rose 'Paul's Scarlet' blends with the popular dark purple Viticella 'Etoile Violette'.

PLATE 118. A rose with many merits, 'New Dawn', will flourish on a north facing wall and still produce fragrant buttonhole roses.

Order of planting

To ensure that the plants have not dried out they would benefit from being immersed in water for a period of about two hours.

The rose or clematis can be extracted from the pot by tapping its edge against the top of a fork stuck into the ground. In the case of a thin plastic pot, this should be cut away. Roses on their bare roots are simply extracted from the protective material.

First put the chosen material in the root layer – layer one. Cover with a thin coating of soil or peat to make the barrier layer – layer two. In the case of the rose and large-bloomed hybrids, gently spread the roots over the surface of the barrier area. In the case of species clematis, on no account touch the thread-like roots. Now fill in with what you have chosen for the plant area – layer three, and the blanket layer – layer four, leave a saucer layer at the top – layer five.

Firm the material around and above the plant with your foot. If a cane is not used then mark the planting area with a short cane or stick which will prevent the clematis or rose, once planted, from getting lost. Attach a label nearby.

Roses and clematis should be planted at least 24in. (60cm.) apart.

Support

The Climbing Rose can be immediately attached to its support. Shrub and Bedding Roses need no support.

The stems of the clematis plant usually arrive from the nursery attached to a cane. Ensure that the stems are firmly attached to the cane and, if necessary, use new ties.

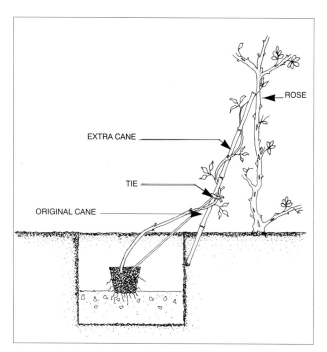

Figure 38. Original cane from nursery can be tied to a new cane

Figure 39. A clematis may be strengthened by carrying its stem through the planting material to its support in the hope that it will root at the stem node

This cane helps support the stem during planting. Once the plant is safely in the hole this cane, if long enough, can carry the stem to a wall, post, host plant or other support. After planting, if the cane is too short, use a new cane of the desired length, insert this near the original cane and tie the old cane to the new. The stem will happily climb from the old cane to the new and onwards to the wall, post, host plant, or other climbing support (see Figure 38).

Producing more stems

Clematis can suffer from clematis wilt which can kill the stem right down to ground level. As an insurance it is useful to encourage the plant to have a number of nodes below ground level so that new stems can arise from them. If one stem succumbs to clematis wilt then the others will survive and the more stems the better. The stem can be detached from the cane after planting and led through the blanket area to a cane near the wall or close to the host plant or support (see Figure 39). There is usually a node in this long stem which will root, giving added strength to the plant. Sometimes the stem is long enough to make a circuit in the hole before it is led to the support. In this event two or three nodes may find themselves below root level, to the advantage of the plant.

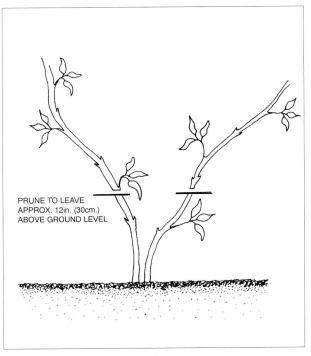

Figure 40. Severe pruning of young plants

PRUNE TO LEAVE APPROX. 12in. (30cm.) ABOVE GROUND LEVEL

Autumn delivered clematis

When clematis are ordered by post in spring they are often delivered in the autumn. It is convenient for nurseries to deliver plants in the autumn as, understandably, they do not want to hold them over the winter. Spring is a better season for planting as the soil is warmer and this is the time when the plant naturally wants to make growth. The clematis delivered in the autumn can be repotted (see later) into a larger pot which is put into a trench in a sheltered position. During this time the roots will make considerable growth and the clematis can then be planted in the spring.

The Evergreen Clematis, as they are tender, should be planted in the late spring.

The first two years for clematis

Care during this period, more than at any other time, guarantees the growth of a fine clematis plant. The gardener should concentrate less on producing bloom than on producing a healthy plant.

Early pruning is required. In the case of the Large Flowered Clematis, wait for one month so that the plant can be fully established in the garden and then inspect the stem, looking for two good buds about 12in. (30cm.) above the ground. Pinch out the stems above the buds (see Figure 40) to reduce the amount of foliage which will reduce the strain on the roots; it will also encourage new shoots to appear. As the new shoots make growth of about 12in. (30cm.), pinch out again above the buds. Continuing to do this you will end up with a nicely branched plant. Should you be so fortunate as to have two stems coming from the base, then the same

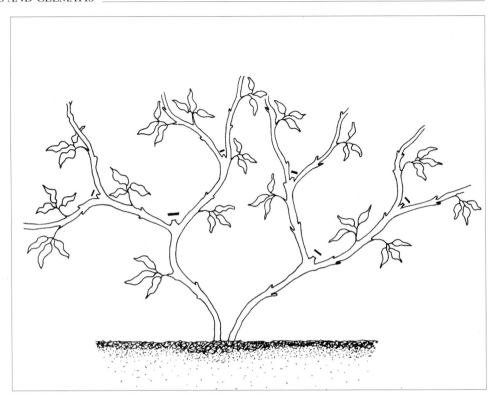

Figure 41. Keep
pinching out the
clematis stem every
12in. (30cm.) to produce
a branching plant

treatment is given to both stems, with one stem veered to the left and the other veered to the right (see figure 41).

In the first two years care must be exercised to water sufficiently. Each plant must receive at least 2 gallons (10 litres) of water per week.

A rich fertiliser is not required in the first year as the plant is going to be given sufficient nutrient in the soil. However, liquid fertiliser should be applied once a week during the growing period. During the second year more fertiliser can be given.

Clematis plants are most susceptible to wilt during their first two years. When woody stems develop the risk becomes much less. Therefore, carefully watch the plants for wilt and, if necessary, take action according to the instructions given later.

Planting near walls
The soil near walls is usually poor. Furthermore, rain may not reach the soil and the wall itself extracts water from the soil. Thus roses and clematis should be planted at least 1½ft. (45cm.) or preferably 2ft. (60cm.) away from the wall.

However, there are times when it is not possible to do this and the rose or clematis has to be planted very close to the wall. This can be successfully achieved by treating the plant as if it were growing in a container.

Excavate the old poor soil and replace with new soil. Line the wall with slates or plastic sheeting to prevent it absorbing water. Great care must be taken to ensure that the area receives sufficient water. It will require the equivalent of 1in. (2.5cm.) of water per week, i.e. 2 gallons (10 litres) of water per plant per week as a minimum. In hot weather it may be necessary to give 2 gallons (10 litres) of water twice a week. Furthermore, attention should be paid to ensure that plants do not dry out during the winter as the rainfall may not reach plants growing close to walls.

PLATE 119. The rose 'Casino' lightens the lovely clematis 'Victoria' with points of yellow colour.

Moving plants

Plants should be moved from one part of the garden to another in the late autumn, winter or early spring when conditions are favourable, i.e. when the soil is not frozen or waterlogged.

If the soil is poor it should be given the treatment mentioned earlier.

When moving a rose it may be desirable to remove some of the top growth so as to make less demand on the roots.

When moving the clematis, again it is better to remove most of the top growth. Care must be taken not to cut into the old woody stems of the clematis as these should be retained with some of the non-woody ones.

In the new site the rose or clematis is planted as described earlier.

POTTING AND REPOTTING

Potting Mixtures

Many proprietary mixtures are available for seeds, seedlings, and mature plants with some based on peat, coir, bark and soil.

If in doubt use the well-established John Innes soil based mixtures with strengths varying from 1-3.

You can mix your own. One recommendation is 65% peat and the rest equal amounts of grit and bark. It must be sterilised.

One expert uses one-third clay, one-third sand, one-third loam; the clay and sand come from deep deposits likely to be sterile.

To whichever mixture you choose add slow release fertiliser - at the agent's recommended strength.

Clematis pots and wind

How can you provide support to container-grown clematis, which can so easily be knocked over by the wind? These potted clematis may be awaiting planting or are being moved between a nursery area and a conservatory. If two strong poles are placed at a distance from one another, a wire can be strung between them. The canes of the individual clematis pots can then be tied to this wire and they will survive any amount of buffeting from wind (see Figure 43).

Repotting (see Figure 42)

1. First, put some compost into a large pot, then place the small pot (with the clematis) inside the large pot to see if both edges are level. If not, add more peat or compost at the bottom until the edge of the inner pot is level with that of the edge of the outer one.

Figure 42. Repotting made easy

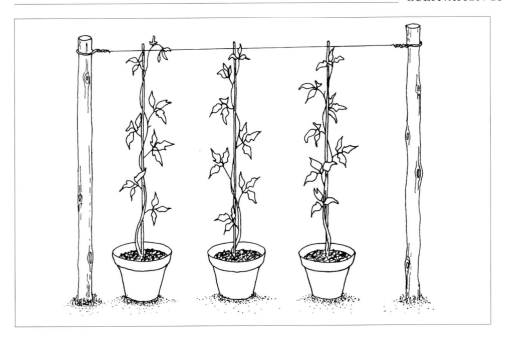

Figure 43. Clematis grown in pots can be protected from the wind by tying the tops of their canes to a wire fixed between posts, as shown

2. Add compost all round the small pot, firming it down gently until the large pot is filled to the brim.

3. You now take the small pot out from inside the large one.

4. Holding the small pot with the clematis in the left hand, slip the base of the stems between the fingers of your right hand, invert the pot and cane, tap the pot edge gently on the edge of a bench or on the top of a fork stuck in the ground (or tap edge of pot with a stick).

5. The clematis will immediately slip out of its pot.

6. The clematis will now fit perfectly into the space previously made in the larger pot. Gently firm and the job is done.

Traditionally, it is usual to repot by using a sequence of pots of increasing size. This practice is now being questioned as, after an initial hesitation, plants grow quickly and well in large pots.

Winter protection

Both roses and clematis are very hardy and only need protection in extreme conditions.

Roses can be protected with a mulch of manure, bark chippings, straw, conifer prunings, etc. In very cold countries the mulch will prevent the frozen ground from thawing as it is during thawing and re-freezing that the damage is done.

Stems can be protected with a circular layer of netting, wire netting, or hessian sacking stuffed with leaves, straw or bracken (see Plate 121). Another method is to wrap the stems in a layer of horticultural fleece.

To protect plants on a wall hang a sheet of hessian sacking in front of them. Alternatively, hang netting in front of the plants and stuff with insulating material.

In spring a sharp frost can damage the buds of the Alpinas, Macropetalas and especially the Montanas which, in turn, may prevent the development of flowers. If the event can be anticipated protect the plant with netting, hessian sacking or horticultural fleece.

The winter protection of containers was discussed earlier (see Chapter 10, page 125).

PLATE 120. The *Clematis heracleifolia* var. 'Mrs Robert Brydon' is an Herbaceous Clematis that can be split in the winter.

Regular Inspection

Plants should be visited at least once a week. There may be signs of early disease that responds best to early treatment. Stems of roses of clematis may need guiding in the best direction or may need tying in. Lack of water can be immediately remedied.

WATERING

In theory it is possible to overwater as a hose directed continually at a piece of ground will ultimately leach all the nutrients out of it. With the amounts

PLATE 121. This delicate clematis is cosy and well-protected in a wire cage filled with oak leaves.

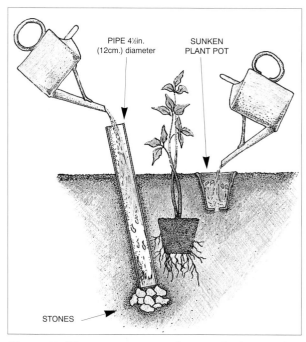

Figure 44. Plant watering is made easier by burying a plant pot or inserting a pipe

PLATE 122. The rose 'New Dawn' and clematis 'Gipsy Queen' make reliable companions into late summer.

recommended here this is unlikely to happen and, in any event, is likely to be counterbalanced by the rich feeding programme.

Newly planted roses and clematis require a minimum of 1 gallon (5 litres) of water a week.

The importance of giving clematis sufficient water cannot be overestimated. Clematis will take up to 4 gallons (20 litres) per plant per week and in hot weather will relish 1 gallon (5 litres) per plant per day.

To be sure that you can exactly determine how much water a plant is having it is best to 'point' the water, i.e. to direct the water specifically on to the plant rather than to allow it to take its share from a general garden watering.

Watering should take place out of the sun in the evening. Watering will, of course, be assisted by having planted your rose or clematis correctly with a saucer area at the top of the hole. The following methods of watering can be used:

1. Watering can. Hard work but it is easy to measure the amount each plant gets.
2. By hose. Use a fine spray both sides of the leaves.
3. Generalised watering. Watering by using a sprayer.
4. During planting, the opportunity can be taken to insert a watering tube into the soil. The aim is to lead the water straight to the root area. A pipe of 4½in. (12cm.) diameter and 15in. (38cm.) long will do the job. At the bottom end of the tube there should be a few stones to allow easy drainage. An alternative watering aid is to sink an empty plant pot close to the clematis and water through this (see Figure 44). With this system put two-thirds of the water into the pipe or pot and the rest over the soil to keep moist any roots which are near to the surface.

A liquid fertiliser can be used at the same time as watering, either by being dissolved in the watering can or served from an attachment added to the hose.

The best watering system

The author is impressed with the leaking, seeping or porous pipe systems. These systems are easy to instal. Do a small area first and you will soon become accustomed to the fittings and method of installation. Once installed the saving of time is enormous and quickly repays the cost and effort. The pipe can be put below the surface and the water goes to the exact spot that you planned to receive it –without wastage. It is easy to control the amount of water the plants receive but make sure the clematis is close to the pipe.

Mulching

The main reason for using a mulch with roses and clematis is to retain the moisture in the ground. This is much more effective than planting the roots in the shade or planting dwarf shrubs around them.

Additional reasons for using a mulch are it keeps the ground cool, suppresses weeds, adds humus to the ground and will also help to add nutrients to the soil. If sterilised mulch material is used, peat for example, then it may help to protect the plant against wilt as it will not contain spores of the fungi.

The mulch should be applied in the spring after the soil has warmed up. Remove any dead material from the ground and burn it. Later, inorganic fertilisers or liquid fertilisers can be applied through the mulch. The fertiliser should be watered in.

Apply sufficient mulch material to cover 2sq. ft. (60 sq. cm.) around the plant and to a thickness of at least 2-3in. (5-8cm.); 3-4in. (8-10cm.) will be even better. Do not carry the mulch material close to the stems as some types, especially fresh manure, can damage the stems (see Figure 45).

In the autumn the mulch material can be forked gently into the ground or left to protect the roots against severe weather.

The following materials can be used:

1. Moist peat. This contains only a little nitrogen and, as it tends toward acidity, it is good for alkaline soils.
2. Mushroom compost. This is often sterile. It is alkaline and therefore particularly good for acid soil. It should not be used if acidity needs to be retained for other plants. Despite its alkalinity, mushroom compost has not been found to be satisfactory with clematis.
3. Leaf mould contains some nutrients. It is usually acid and an excellent mulching material.
4. Farmyard manure tends to be acid. An excellent mulching material but the manure must be old and so cut like cake.
5. Garden compost. Tends to be acid and an excellent mulching material.
6. Well rotted straw or sawdust.
7. Grass clippings. Tends to take the nitrogen out of the soil.

Figure 45. The introduction of a thick layer of mulch (not less than 2ft. (60cm.) square around the clematis is beneficial. The material used should not come into contact with the plant stems

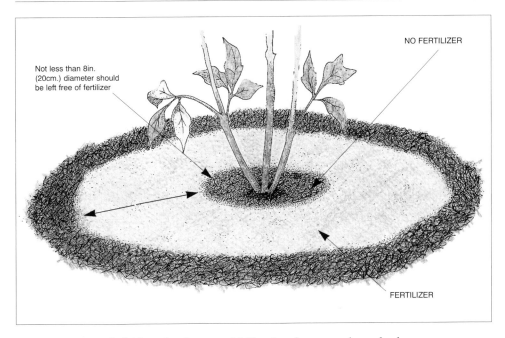

Not less than 8in. (20cm.) diameter should be left free of fertilizer

NO FERTILIZER

FERTILIZER

Figure 46. Keep artificial fertilizers away from clematis plants to avoid possible stem rot. Leave an area free of fertilizer near the stems

Not recommended if a selective weed killer has been used on the lawn.

8. Pulverised bark. Contains few nutrients.

9. Black polythene sheeting, or pole sheeting, with a hole in the sheeting from which the plant emerges. Can be disguised with bark or stones.

10. Porous sheeting which prevents weeds coming through, retains water in the soil and, at the same time being porous, allows water and fertilisers to pass through easily.

11. As a last resort stones, small bricks or shingle can also be used.

If materials which are liable to take nitrogen out of the soil are being used then 2-3oz. (60-90 g.) of sulphate of ammonia can be spread over the ground to 1 sq. yd. (1 sq. m.) before applying the mulch.

Plants can, of course, be used to create shade but they also tend to take water and nutrients out of the ground. The most suitable plants to use for shade are pansies, primulas, dwarf lavenders and the small potentillas.

If roses and clematis are planted in holes in stone material as, for example, on a patio, then they will flourish because the stonework acts as a mulch material. Naturally the soil in the hole must be well-supplied with humus, nutrients, and water.

Feeding

In a good loamy soil little or no fertilising will be necessary. Many soils, however, will need feeding.

Manure and garden compost give invaluable humus to the soil, improve drainage and the retention of water.

Most energy must be given to the plants, however, in the form of fertilisers. These should be used according to recommended strength, spread evenly and uniformly about the plant and moved gently into the soil by fork, hand or hoe.

Peat, although it contains no nourishment, is a good mulch and a soil conditioner; if used, it should be strengthened by containing an artificial fertiliser.

It is most important to ensure that manure, compost and artificial compost are spread well away from the stems of the plant – to a distance of 4in. (10cm.). Most of the roots are spread widely below and the fertiliser will reach them better away from the stem. Another important reason is that young manure and artificial fertiliser will rot the stems and even kill a plant (see Figure 46).

Foliar feeding may be time-consuming but used once a week, at recommended strength, it is an excellent way of boosting your choice plants. It is especially helpful with young roses and clematis. It is usually possible to undertake the foliar feeding with the watering programme.

Suggested Feeding Schedule

In the autumn
1 Apply bonemeal at the rate of 3½oz. (100g.) per sq. yd. (per sq. m.). Bonemeal is a slow release fertiliser and will still be at work in the following spring and longer. It tends to make the ground alkaline, is rich in phosphates and encourages root growth. It should be worked gently into the ground.
In light ground the bonemeal may attract ants and should be replaced with a general fertiliser.
2. Provide a mulch of garden compost or well-rotted manure. Spread it to about 2ft. (60cm.) around the plant. The manure must be well-rotted.
3. In very cold areas the mulch of protective material may need to be spread around the plant.

In the spring
1. Gently dig in the autumn manure.
2. Add a handful of potash or artificial fertiliser rich in potash. Water it into the soil.
3. Now apply another mulch of suitable material or manure.
4. Apply a liquid fertiliser rich in potash once a week if possible. A well-established plant will need the benefit of liquid feed twice a week. Never apply the fertiliser stronger than stated in the instructions – 'little and often' is the secret to success. Water first if the soil is dry. Stop the liquid fertiliser when the rose or clematis is in flower as it will shorten the flowering period.

In midsummer
1. Give another handful of potash or a fertiliser rich in potash. Water it in. This will help the second flowering of the clematis and rose.
2. Continue the liquid feeding as above.

LABELLING

The ideal label shows the name clearly, is easily visible, is permanent and yet not obtrusive. It is very difficult, with any label, to achieve all these requirements.

Roses and clematis should be labelled at the time of planting, but the label should not be fixed on the plant as neither rose nor clematis likes the label attached, especially if it is metal. Labels attached to plants can also disappear at the time of pruning! Thus the label should be attached to either the support of the rose (wall, post, etc.) or be put into the ground nearby. If the latter, however, they can impede hoeing and may be rendered invisible by weeds.

If the roses (Shrub and Bedding) and clematis are in a bed away from a support the label cannot be put on it but must go into the ground or be fixed to the pole supporting the plant. Sometimes a short stick may have to be fixed specially into the ground to support the label.

As has been said earlier, there are so many hazards with labels that it is imperative

PLATE 123. The rose 'Danse du Feu' tries to steal the show from clematis 'Perle d'Azur'.

PLATE 124. The rose 'Pink Perpétue' combines with clematis 'Victoria' before a cottage window.

to have a plan showing the position of each rose and clematis. This plan can be consulted in the winter months and the correctness of the labels checked. Defective labels can be put right for the growing season.

The most durable forms of labels tend to be the most expensive. The cheapest label is a white or coloured plastic piece with the name of the plant in so-called 'permanent' ink. Experience shows that the plastic piece becomes fragile after a season and the 'permanent' ink is hardly visible after two seasons at most. Thus it is necessary to replace most labels every year after checking with the plan of planting. White plastic labels do not add to the beauty of the garden and should be tucked out of sight.

Possible labels are:

Solid metal pieces on which are painted the names of plants. Repainting is required every few years. Some have a projection that allows for sticking them into the ground. Paint markers are now available for easier painting and can also be used on the materials below. Names can also be put on Dymo Tape and attached to the metal.

Aluminium labels can be hung on supports or stuck into the ground on legs. These have a special pencil for writing the name. They are expensive but it is claimed that marking is permanent (probably lasts for some seasons). Aluminium labels are also available at more cost where a puncher indents the name on the label. A permanent solution - although weathering takes its toll.

Zinc labels can be hung on supports or stuck into the ground on legs. A special pen is used for writing the name. They are expensive but robust.

Copper labels can be hung on supports or stuck into the ground on legs. The name is scratched on the copper. 'Scratching' is said to give permanency to the naming. A ball point pen will work with some copper labels. However, weathering tends to make the whole label difficult to see.

Plastic of various sizes in white or green can be attached to supports or stuck into the ground. The name is put on the label with 'permanent' inking. They are cheap but need replacing after two seasons at most. Recently, black-coated plastic labels have become available on which names are scratched with a scriber.

Pottery labels are attractive but expensive.

Pebbles, on which is discreetly painted the name of the plant, are an attractive option.

Other expensive options are using an electric engraver to write names on a metal surface or having heavy duty aluminium or zinc labels 'machine engraved' to order from a commercial outlet.

PRUNING ROSES

Roses should be pruned in early or mid spring, depending on the climate of the area in which the garden lies.

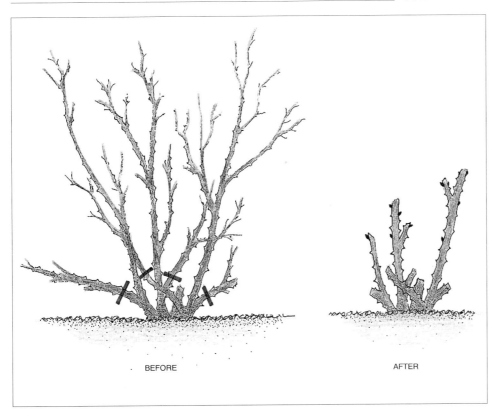

BEFORE

AFTER

Figure 47. Pruning a bush rose

Pruning of young plants

As with clematis, it is advantageous to prune young bush roses to about 6-8in. (15-20cm.) from the ground and, at their strongest, 5in. (12 cm.) from the ground. Shrub and Climbing Roses should be pruned to about three times as long.

Bush Roses

Step 1. Cut out all dead wood.

Step 2. Cut out all weak shoots.

Step 3. If there are a number of stems, cut out one or two stems at the centre of the plant to open it out and to let light in.

Step 4. Cut the remaining stems hard, if it is desired to have a small number of large blooms, leaving, say, 4-6in. (10-15cm.).

Step 5. Cut the stems less hard if more flowers are required for bedding purposes leaving, say, 10-12in. (25-30cm.) (see Figure 47).

Make a sloping cut with secateurs above a bud (see Figure 48).

Experiments at The Royal National Rose Society in England are suggesting that very good results are obtained with less strict pruning. Good results were obtained by using a hedge trimmer on the bushes!

Bedding Roses in exposed windy areas may need some of their stems cut off in the autumn to reduce wind resistance.

Bedding Roses may thus have three prunings:

In the spring to encourage flowering.

In the summer (dead heading) to encourage a further crop.

In the autumn to reduce wind resistance.

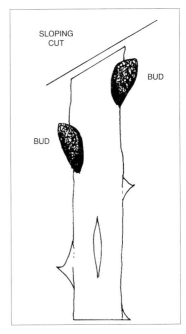

SLOPING CUT

BUD

BUD

Figure 48. Making a sloping cut

PLATE 125. Rose 'Summer Wine' and Polish clematis 'Blue Angel' are companions of equal delicate beauty.

Shrub Roses

Cut out all the dead wood.

Shorten the remaining stems to about a third of their length.

Every two years cut out a main stem to encourage the Shrub to throw up new main stems. If growth becomes poor resort to removing more main stems although it may not flower well the first year after drastic pruning.

Climbing Roses

These need little pruning.

Step 1. Cut out all dead shoots.

Step 2. Cut out all weak shoots.

Step 3. If they are weak, trim the remaining side shoots close to the main shoot. Stronger side shoots should not be trimmed so close. Very strong side shoots should be left as they are.

Step 4. If a main stem has become old and unproductive of flowers cut it out. This will encourage new main stems to rise from the base. This may not need to be done every year.

Step 5. Stems should be fanned out downwards and outwards so that when the shoots flower or make growth they will shoot upwards and cover the wall of a fence (see Figure 49).

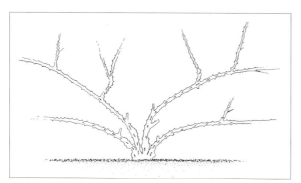

Figure 49. With climbers fan stems downwards and outwards

The pruning of Climbing Roses can be undertaken in the autumn.

PLATE 126. The viticella 'Abundance', true to its name, climbs high into the rose
'Parkdirektor Riggers'.

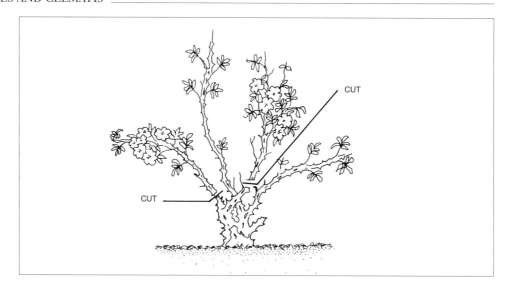

Figure 50. With some ramblers the stems that flowered this year should be cut out at their base

Ramblers
1. Some Ramblers, for example, 'Emily Grey' need very little pruning.
2. Some Ramblers, with similar habits to Climbers, for example, 'New Dawn' should be pruned as for the Climbers above.
3. If the Rambler is the type which throws up strong stems from the base each year then the old wood which has flowered should be cut away in the autumn. The young, new, green stems are then tied to the support. 'American Pillar' is a type requiring this treatment (see Figure 50).

Dead-heading
Bedding, Climbing, and some Shrub Roses will profit from dead-heading i.e. the removal of spent flowers. Cut off the pieces of the stem with the spent flowers – as if pruning. Remove anything from 6-18in. (15-45cm.). As this is done in the summer it amounts to a summer pruning and will encourage the roses to send up new shoots with new roses giving an additional crop later. Another school of thought says that equally good results are obtained by snapping off the dead blooms.

Clematis
The pruning of clematis is easy if the following four principles are understood.
1. The earlier the clematis flowers the less pruning it requires while the later the clematis flowers the more pruning it requires.
2. There are three pruning types according to the seasons.
I.   Early Season Flowering. **No pruning.**
II. Mid Season Flowering. **Light pruning**.
III. Late Season Flowering. **Severe pruning.**
3. If we understand the differences between types II and III above we can understand why they are pruned differently.
Type II clematis such as 'Nelly Moser' make flowers on stems made the previous year. If we prune off these stems we will get no flowers. Hence the light pruning.
Type III clematis such as 'Jackmanii' flower on stems grown this year. If we prune severely in the spring we will encourage more new stems to grow and will get more flowers. Hence the severe pruning.
4. It will help if we remember the following:
When pruning Type II start at the **top** and work **down**.
When pruning Type III start at the **bottom** and work **up**.

Type I. The Early Small Flowered Clematis (Five groups – Evergreen, Alpina, Macropetala, Montana and Rockery).
NO PRUNING, just a tidy (see Figure 51).
In late spring/early summer, after flowering, cut the shoots to tidy the plant so it fits comfortably into the space you are giving it. With experience you will know how much growth it will make in the year and you will prune back so as to allow the plant to grow during the season to the confines of the space you have given it.

Type II. Early Large Flowered Hybrids (One group).
LIGHT PRUNING (see Figure 52).
In the late winter/early spring trim out the dead stems.

Start at the TOP of each stem and work DOWN to an outward pointing, healthy pair of buds. Prune the shoots above the buds and as they are high up you should not be taking much away. If, on the other hand, you have a tangled mass at the top, prune just below it.
Fan the remainder out.
If you have the time you can also give this type a light pruning, after they have flowered, to encourage them to give you another crop late in the season.

Type III. Late Flowering Clematis (Six groups: Late Large Flowered, Herbaceous, Viticella, Texensis, Orientalis and Late Species)
SEVERE PRUNING (see Figure 53).

In late winter/early spring start at the BOTTOM and work UP on each stem until you find a strong pair of buds. Cut above the buds. The buds may be as low as 3-12in. (8-30cm.) from the ground. If you happen to cut to the ground, do not worry, a new shoot will appear from the soil.
In the Orientalis Group there is a choice. Light pruning will give early blooming. Severe pruning will give more and larger flowers - but later.

Pruning Clematis

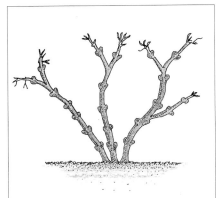

Figure 51. No pruning. Tidy after blooming

Figure 52. Light pruning.
1. Start at TOP
2. Work DOWN stems
3. Cut above first strong pair of buds high up on stems

Figure 53. Severe pruning
1. Start at BOTTOM
2. Work UP stems
3. Cut above pair of strong buds low down on stems

PLATE 127. The glowing Climbing Rose 'Super Star' climbs with the vigorous cheerful Viticella 'Mme Julia Correvon'.

Extra Points on Pruning

1. Use secateurs or scissors, depending on the toughness of the shoots.

2. Always burn shoots at once after pruning. This will reduce the risk of leaving spores of wilt around.

3. Never cut into strong, woody stems. Clematis do not like it and the plant is liable to give up the ghost. The green stems of young plants become brown and firm after two to three years and more green stems grow from the woody stem. These green stems are the ones to prune.

4. If the Late Flowering Clematis (Type III) look a mess in the autumn, perhaps on Ground Cover Roses, hard prune them back as they will come to no harm. If on a Climbing Rose, undo the ties, tug, and it will all come away. Prune to 2-3ft. (60-90cm.) from the ground and if the shoots are tied together they will be unobtrusive. It is wise not to prune to the ground then as the remaining stems will protect the crown of the plant through the winter.

5. If after a few years your Type II, Early Large Flowered Group become rather a tangled mass, cut them down, after flowering, below the tangle, even if you are down to a short distance from the ground. Do not, however, cut into the thick woody stems. Your clematis will make new growth by the end of the year and produce good blooms the next season. This is a technique that you may have to employ every few years if you do not have the time for annual pruning.

6. If in any doubt as to which group a clematis belongs to check the name in the list of the catalogue of any clematis nursery. They always show the pruning type.

PLATE 128. English Rose 'Heritage' and clematis 'Lasurstern' make a colourful combination.

7. If you make an error do not despair.
If you prune the early clematis severely then they will simply flower later.
If you give little pruning to the Late Flowering Clematis then it simply means they will be less productive than they might have been and will be rather straggly at the base.
If you forget to prune entirely then you should still find a reasonable display of blooms.
8. If you do not know which group a plant belongs to let it grow a year and it will become apparent.
9. Occasionally you will need a clematis to grow to an unusual height on a pergola. The Late Large Flowering Clematis and the Viticella Sub-group are good for this. Over two to three years prune 3-4ft. (90-110cm.) from the ground. The low stems will soon become brown and hard and put out green shoots on which the flowers appear. You have now raised above ground level by 3-4ft. (90-110cm.). Always prune the green shoots which arise from the brown ones.

Dead-heading
Most authorities are agreed that clematis benefit from dead-heading in the first two years of their growth. Some even state that mature plants will also profit from dead-heading as it encourages new growth and hence more flowers.

Table of Pruning Requirements

The pruning requirements of each of the twelve groups of clematis are shown in the following table. If you know which group your clematis belongs to then the table will tell you the pruning requirement. The clematis are listed according to approximate time of flowering.

PRUNING REQUIREMENTS OF THE TWELVE CLEMATIS GROUPS		
Group	**Example**	**Pruning**
Evergreen	'Armandii'	No Pruning
Alpina	'Frances Rivis'	No Pruning
Macropetala	'Markhamii'	No Pruning
Montana	'Mayleen'	No Pruning
Rockery	'Marmoraria'	No Pruning
Early Large Flowered	'Nelly Moser'	Light Pruning
Late Large Flowered	'Jackmanii'	Severe Pruning
Herbaceous	*C. integrifolia* 'Rosea'	Severe Pruning
Viticella	'Mme Julia Correvon'	Severe Pruning
Texensis	'Gravetye Beauty'	Severe Pruning
Orientalis	'Bill Mackenzie'	Severe Pruning
Late Species	'Flammula'	Severe Pruning

DISEASES AND PESTS

ROSES
The main ones are as follows:

Fungal

Black spot - roundish dark spots on upper leaf surface leading to yellowing and loss of leaves.
Prevent by spraying with a systematic fungicide every month from late spring - mid autumn. Prune out and burn affected leaves.
Effective fungicides include Bupirimate-Triforine (Nimrod-T), Thiophanate-Methyl (Systemic fungicide, M&B; Topsin-M), Mycloputanil (Bio-Systhane) and Propiconazole, Carbendazim (Bio-super carb.), Mancozeb (Bio-Dithane 945) and copper with ammonium hydroxide (Spraydex).

Powdery Mildew - white or grey powdery patches on young leaves. Spray as soon as seen. Spray again one week later. Results are very good with modern fungicides such as the above.

Rust - common in coastal areas. Orange-yellow pustules on under side of leaflets. These turn black and spores are shed. Leaves wither and die. Stems also affected in bad attack.
Responds to systemic fungicides such as Mancozeb (Bio Dithane 945), Propiconazole, Myclobutanil (Bio Systhane), Bupirimate-Triforine (Nimrod-T). Also remove affected leaves and stems and burn.

Pests

Greenfly - attack in late spring and early summer.

Regularly responds to systemic or contact insecticides which should be applied in late spring before the main crop flowering and again two weeks later. These are also effective against leaf hoppers and capsid bugs.

Insecticides containing the following active agents will be effective - Dimethoate, Malathion, Fenitrulthion, Permethrin, Pirimiphos-Methyl, Pirimicarb. Soap and water is also effective.

CLEMATIS

Clematis are remarkably healthy apart from one serious disease - clematis wilt.

Clematis Wilt (Stem Rot)

Fungi can do good or ill. Penicillin is the product of a good fungus, clematis wilt of a bad. They are always with us, over 60,000 of them.

If you look at life from the point of view of the fungus you realise that, poor thing, it has to wait years in the soil for the right conditions before it can eat and reproduce.

In the case of the clematis wilt fungus the necessary conditions are something like this. It needs the plump green stems of a clematis plant in its first two years when it is about to flower. With the green stems it likes a temperature of about 23°C, humidity, and, if possible, a damaged part of the stem where it can get in.

Once the clematis has grown woody stems in two to three years it is less likely to be attacked as the fungus cannot penetrate them.

The wilt flourishes in a way that does maximum damage quickly - it works right across the stem, killing as it goes, to a length of 1-2 inches. So it cuts off the sap and naturally the plant above the damage will wilt in days. Your leaves and flowers will hang limply, and then turn brown and then black.

Clematis can wilt for other reasons. If you, by accident, cut right across the stem it will wilt. If you do not give it water it will wilt. Vine weevils eating the roots of a clematis will make that plant wilt. So the word 'wilt' does not tell us about the work of the wilt fungus. When I looked at the damage done by the fungus it was clear that this damage was in the nature of a rotting of the stem. So we should call the condition 'stem rot'.

The damage is always at a node, usually low down near the ground. The affected node may have a little slime over it on the outside. Making a clean slice vertically up the stem reveals the damage at one node. A black rotted area extends for ½-1in. (1-2.5cm.), on either side of the node. The lesion extends right across the stem which is why it does so much damage. Below the lesion the stem is green, at the lesion it is black while above it the stem is brown as it dies. The black area becomes dry and powdery (see Plate 129, believed to be the first photograph showing the lesion of clematis wilt or stem rot). A plant should not be assumed to be damaged by clematis wilt (stem rot) unless the lesion has been identified.

'Which fungus is responsible?'

I asked myself that and decided to investigate. To my surprise I found that the fungus *Ascochyta clematidina* had been discovered by W. O. Gloyer in New York State in the USA as far back as 1915 but his findings were largely ignored. Quite recently his work was confirmed in the UK, Holland and New Zealand. The Dutch found

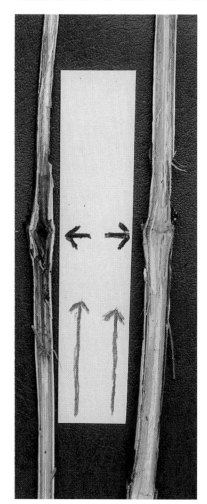

PLATE 129. This photograph illuminates the fungal 'stem rot' (wilt) in clematis. Two clematis nodes (marked with an arrow) are seen here. The right node has healthy green tissue above and below it (the flow from the roots upwards is indicated by red arrows). The left node has healthy green tissue below it but at the node itself this tissue has been destroyed by the fungus leaving a black mass for about 2in. (5cm). Above the left node the tissue is cut off from nourishment by the fungal infection and the tissue turns brown as it dies.

another nasty fungus that did the same job - *Coniothyrium clematidis-recta*.

The next question, was 'Why does 'stem rot' only attack the Large Flowered Clematis? Why are they susceptible?'

These Large Flowered Clematis were developed between 1860 and 1880. Then 'stem rot' appeared and was so devastating in its effects that the nurseries stopped growing clematis.

So how did the weakness come in?

The first Large Flowered Clematis ever, Jackmanii, had the weakness. It was the product of *C. lanuginosa* and *C. viticella*. *C. viticella* we know is immune. So my suspicions fell on *C. lanuginosa*. Whichever clematis was responsible worked on a big scale. Indeed, the whole clematis production of twenty years suffered. *C. lanuginosa* fitted the bill here too as it was very commonly employed in hybridising. So, to check on *C. lanuginosa* seemed sensible.

More work was necessary and, with the help of many knowledgeable clematis growers, it was possible to make lists of clematis that often or rarely wilted.

What was the difference between the two groups?

The first difference was that the big wilters came from the Early Large Flowered Clematis. Examples are (in order of wilting) 'Vyvyan Pennell', 'Countess of Lovelace', 'Mrs N. Thompson', 'Henryi', 'William Kennett', 'Duchess of Edinburgh', 'Mrs Cholmondeley', 'Lawsoniana'. The low wilters came from the Late Flowering Large Flowered Clematis, for example (in order of not wilting), 'Hagley Hybrid', 'Ville de Lyon', 'Gipsy Queen', 'Comtesse de Bouchaud', 'Perle d'Azur', 'Huldine', 'Margot Koster', 'Ernest Markham'.

The second difference emerged when I looked at the ancestry of the two groups. All the big wilters had a heavy loading of *C. lanuginosa* in their pedigree. The low wilters rarely had *C. lanuginosa* in their pedigree. So *C. lanuginosa* is clearly the cause of the weakness.

The final answer to clematis wilt is to hybridise with clematis that have no *C. lanuginosa* in their background.

In the meantime, what does the gardener do?

Fortunately there is a lot that can be done and we do not have to stop growing the Large Flowered Clematis - even beautiful 'Vyvyan Pennell'.

1. Plant your clematis with the top of the roots 4in. (10cm.) below the ground. This will cause a node or two on the stem to be underground. Roots will appear at these nodes. If the main root is ever killed by 'stem rot' then new plants will appear from the nodes. When planting you can even twirl a stem, if it is strong, round in a circle to make sure some nodes are underground.

2. In the first two years spend the time strengthening the plant rather than going

PLATE 130. The beautiful early flowering clematis 'Duchess of Edinburgh' is liable to 'wilting'. Take the precautions described here or replace with the equally beautiful variety 'Arctic Queen' (see Plate 29).

for flowers. Keep nipping the stems back to encourage a good growth of side shoots and, very important, to encourage more stems from the ground. If you then lose one stem from 'stem rot' a number of others will still be left.

3. If 'stem rot' strikes then let the eye travel down the stem until it is below any wilting leaves. This may take you down to near ground level or even below. Cut the stem at this point, collect and burn it. The fungus is often present on the leaves of clematis.

4. Now comes an important point. It is not 'stem rot' that kills the plant, it is usually the gardener because many of them assume the plant is dead and neglect it. Instead, keep watering and in no time new stems will appear. If you are unlucky a plant can wilt a couple of times more but in the end you will have a strong plant.

5. Once your plant has woody brown stems it is unusual for these to be attacked as they have a strong defensive reaction against 'stem rot'. Branch stems, however, can still be affected, as can the leaves. If they are affected, cut them off and burn them.

6. Can you stop a plant wilting altogether?
You can. Fungicides have been developed against 'stem rot'. These include carbendazim (Bio-Supercab Bavistan), thiophanate-methyl in 0.2% suspension

(Topsin M), prochloraz (Sportak, Octave), chlorothalonil (Bravo), Fenpropimorph (Corbel), propiconazole (Tilt), Dichlorfluanide (Eurapen), captafol (Difolatan) and other products with the same active agents.

You can spray the fungicides on the plants but it is better is to use systemic fungicides and put them into the ground. (Also, you will not inhale them.) Give the plant a good watering first then sprinkle the fungicide from a watering can. Water the fungicide into the ground. Start in April. Do it every month until September and you should not get any wilt. One last point. Ring the changes on your fungicide so that the fungus does not develop immunity to it.

Mildew

This tends to occur late in the season and particularly involves the Late Large Flowered Clematis. The Texensis Group are also vulnerable. Leaves and flowers will look as if they are dusted with a disfiguring grey-white powder.

As soon as the mildew is seen apply systemic fungicides which are very effective. In the case of the Texensis Group, it is useful to spray just before the plants flower and again after two weeks. Thiophanate-Methyl (Topsin-M) and Propiconazole (Tilt) are effective against blackspot in roses and clematis wilt.

Pests

Earwigs - the population of earwigs builds towards the late summer and they attack the foliage, the buds and the flowers of clematis, distorting everything. The earwigs can be captured in inverting pots on canes and dropped into a salty water solution or the plants dusted with Gamma HCH (Lindane) powder.

Slugs and Snails

These particularly attack new shoots and can do great damage. Slug bait is partially successful and hiding places can also be sprayed with liquid killer.

Vine Weevil

The grubs of the vine weevil can attack the roots of clematis plants in greenhouses. Carefully inspect the clematis once it is removed from the pot. If any grubs are seen they should be immediately destroyed. If there are signs of extensive damage to roots then the clematis plant should be discarded.

Rabbits and Pheasants

In rural areas these can cause massive damage to young shoots and plants may need to be protected by wire enclosures.

Chemical Programmes

The main fungal diseases of roses and clematis respond to the same fungicides and insecticides and it is possible therefore, to have a combined or joint programme.

Compatibles - these are fungicides and insecticides that can be used together.

Cocktail Sprays - these are ready-mixed fungicides and insecticides that can be used as they are, for example, 'Roseclear', 'Multirose', 'Fillip'.
Contact fungicides and insecticides work by being sprayed on the plant.

Systemic insecticides and fungicides can be used either as a spray or watered into

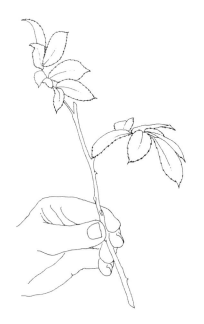

Figure 54. Taking a hard wood rose cutting

Figure 55. The 'trench' method of rooting hard wood cuttings

the ground around the plant. Watering into the ground is easier than spraying and also gets around the problem of possibly inhaling the sprays. The systemics are absorbed by the roots and spread throughout the plants.

PROPAGATION

Roses

Commercially, roses are propagated by budding on to a wild rose, hence the tendency for suckers of the wild rose to appear above the surface in your beds. Complete bud union has to be 1 in. (2.5cm.) below the ground at planting. At one time clematis were propagated by grafting but nowadays they are grown on their own roots. Amateurs can propagate roses in the following two ways:

Hard wood cuttings.

This method applies to strong Floribundas, Ramblers, Climbers and Shrub Roses. It may not work so well with Hybrid Teas. Take the cuttings in late autumn.

1. Take a young shoot from this year's growth and about the thickness of a pencil. Cut just below the bud. Remove the lower leaves and thorns. Retain two leaves at the top. Dip the bottom of the cutting into a rooting compound. The shoot should be about 9in. (23cm.) long. (See Figure 54.)

2. Dig a trench with one vertical wall. The trench should be in semi-shade. Insert the cutting into the trench, ideally into sharp sand. with the leaves above the surface. The cuttings should be about 6in. (15cm.) apart. (See Figure 55.) Replace the soil and make the ground firm by treading it down. Water thoroughly.

Keep the cuttings moist throughout the next year. Rooting takes place in about 28 weeks. In late autumn of the following year the cuttings should be well-rooted and ready for planting.

Using the method described above in midsummer, with special care to keep the cuttings moist, can produce cuttings with roses in eight weeks – but only for Ground Cover and Miniature Roses.

PLATE 131. Late blooming, lovely clematis 'Ville de Lyon' is immune from clematis 'stem rot', as its raiser French grower Morel showed at the turn of the century.

Layering

This method can be used for Ramblers, some Climbing Roses and Shrubs. For success it is essential to have a long flexible stem which will come down to the ground.

1. Layering should be done in mid or late summer.
2. A new plant can be separated from the parent plant in early or mid spring of the following year.
3. Transplant the new plant to its permanent position.
4. Do not allow the plant to flower during its first season.

(For more details on layering see the section below.)

CLEMATIS

Commercially clematis are no longer propagated by grafting but by soft wood cuttings. The amateur can use the following methods:

Layering

This is the best method for producing a small number of clematis plants. The advantages are:

1) The new plant comes true to type, i.e., the off-spring will have the identical characteristics of the parent.

2) This method can be used to extend an existing plant on one or both sides thus creating a larger impact. Furthermore, should the original plant die there will be replacement ones.

3) The layered plant can be used elsewhere in the garden.

Layering can begin as soon as the ground gets warm in early spring.

This method can be used with both the Large Flowered and Small Flowered varieties. In the case of the Late Large Flowering hybrids, the Jackmanii Group, some stems can be left unpruned during the spring pruning, brought down to ground level and used for layering.

Although layering can be done at any time until the autumn, the plants may not be ready until the following year. Spring layered plants will have formed roots by the

PLATE 132. The rose 'Pink Perpétue' is a fine companion to the purple Viticella 'Etoile Violette'.

autumn and be ready for potting up.

With many of the strong growing clematis it is possible to use a simple method. Just bring a clematis stem down to the ground, make a trench 4-6in. (10-15cm.) deep with your hand or trowel, gently lay the stem in the trench, place the soil over it, place a brick over each node and fix the end of the stem to a cane. Keep the stem well-watered. Using a simple method like this probably means you will attempt to layer many more clematis.

A more exact method is as follows (see Figure 56, page 176):

1. A long stem is gently brought down towards the ground. Old material, not green material, is best for layering.

2. Carefully inspect the stem to see where there are good nodes. With a sharp knife, cut below the node joint, slicing upwards about half-way through the joint to make a short 'tongue'. To keep the 'tongue' open slip a matchstick or pebble in the elbow.

3. Powder the joint with hormone rooting powder.

4. With a trowel make a trench 4-6in. (10-15cm.) deep. Place peat and soil or potting compost and soil or sharp sand in the trench. Gently peg the node down into this mixture using a piece of wire bent into the shape of a hairpin. Cover the node with the mixture.

5. Cover the node with a good mulch and a brick or stones to keep the area moist.

6. Mark the end of the stem with a short cane to remind you where the layer is and to fix the stem.

7. Water freely and keep watered.

8. Leave for six to twelve months. To test whether you have roots, gently pull the end of the stem – if there is resistance you have roots.

9. With secateurs, sever the layered plant from the parent plant, gently lift with a fork and pot up immediately. Do not let the roots dry out. Water the pot and give it liquid fertiliser feed. When the plant is strong it can be planted out.

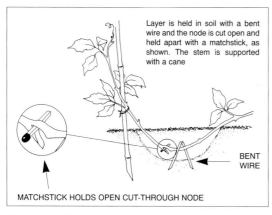

Figure 56. Layering clematis

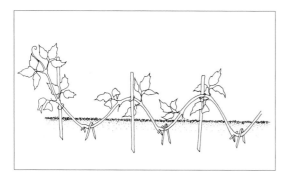

Figure 57. Serpentine layering either into soil or a series of pots – otherwise, as above

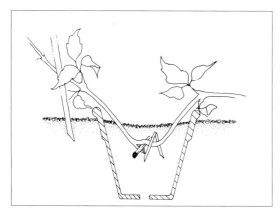

Figure 58. Layering as above but into a pot

Serpentine layering

This involves taking a particularly long shoot and a number of nodes. Each of the nodes is treated as described earlier. Part of the stem between nodes is above ground (see Figure 57). Nodes can be in the ground or in pots in the ground.
Instead of putting the node into a trench it can be gently laid into a mixture in a 10in. (25cm.) pot. The mixture can be soil-based potting compost, or peat and soil, or compost and soil (see Figure 58).

Division

This applies particularly to herbaceous plants (see Plate 120) which are easy to divide. It can be applied to other well-established plants with care and should be done in early spring using a sharp knife.

The pieces of plant are put straight into the ground prepared for clematis or, if they are small, planted in pots and later, when they are large enough, planted outside.

Nibbling

Nibbling is different from root division. In nibbling the parent plant remains in the ground. Careful observation reveals, especially in established plants, that the spread of the plant is so wide that it should be possible to nibble at it and take a piece away. You may even see an extension close to an established plant. Sometimes an established plant is so broad that it is possible to nibble away at two or three corners of it.
The golden rule of nibbling is that one must never risk damaging the parent plant.

The roots of clematis go very deep, and a sharp spade must be placed therefore, between the parent plant and the portion to be nibbled. The spade must be driven deep into the ground separating the roots of the nibbled portion from that of the main plant. It is then withdrawn and driven in again in three places to complete a square around the portion to be nibbled.

By pushing the spade in on the most convenient side, the nibbled part is then taken out of the ground.

The nibbled portion, if large enough, can be grown in a prepared hole as usual.

If a small portion, it can be potted into a large pot and then 'grown on' for another year.

Soft Wood Cuttings

The Small Flowered Clematis will do best by this method as will certain vigorous Large Flowered varieties. The new plant will, of course, be true to type and will have the same characteristics as the parents.
Proceed as follows:

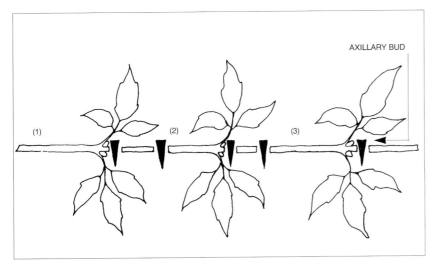

Figure 59. Three inter-nodal cuttings

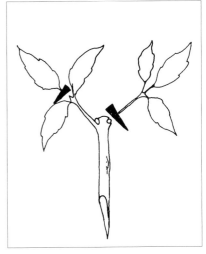

Figure 61. Nodal cutting, which will root from the lower node, has its leaves trimmed off. New leaves will appear from the upper axillary buds

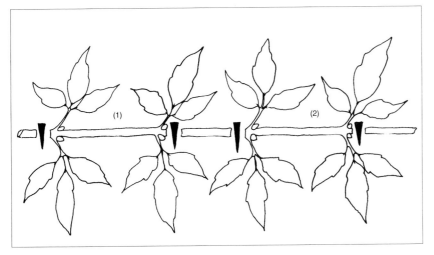

Figure 60. Two nodal cuttings

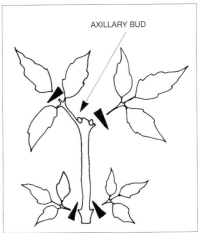

Figure 62. Trimming off leaves

1. The sooner the cuttings are taken in the spring the longer time they will have to become good, strong plants before the autumn. Check your plants to see if stems have been produced from which it will be suitable to take cuttings. Cuttings must be taken from stems which are firm and semi-hard. This usually means that the tip of the stem will produce cuttings which are too soft while the bottom part produces those which are too hard. The middle stem, therefore, may be the most suitable and the ideal cutting is one firm enough to slip into the cutting mixture with a firm push.
2. The potting mixture for the cutting should be half moss peat and half grit. Others advocate two parts sharp sand and one part peat or use soil-based cuttings compost. The mixture should be sterilized.
3. An inter-nodal cutting is taken (find a node with its leaves, then cut between this node and the one below). Thus there is only a node at the top end of the cutting. The total length of the cutting should be between 1-2in. (2.5-5cm.) (see Figure 59). Should you come across a clematis with its nodes very close together then you may

PLATE 133. It is uncommon for a chance seedling to produce a gardenworthy plant. Lovely, delicate 'Louise Rowe' was an exception.

need to use a nodal cutting. There will be a node at the top and the bottom end of the cutting (see Figures 60 and 61, page 177).

4. Spread the clematis stem on a bench and make the cuttings with a sharp knife or razor blade. Keep the cuttings moist and use at once.

5. Trim off completely one set of the pair of leaves. The leaf that remains can also have its central leaflet cut off (see Figure 62, page 177).

6. Quickly dip the cutting in water and then into hormone rooting powder, allowing a dip of about 1in. (2.5cm.) of the stem.

7. Gently but firmly push the cutting into the compost in the pot until the buds are resting on its surface. Avoid the cuttings coming into contact with one another. The cuttings should be 3in. (8cm.) apart with the leaves not touching each other, the compost or the pot's cover. Label the pot.

8. Spray the pot with water containing a fungicide. Let the pot drain. The type of fungicide used should be changed every ten days.

9. Put the pot into either a propagator, a cold frame, or a pot covered with polythene. In the latter event, place four stakes at the circumference of the pot, to keep the polythene away from the leaves (see Figure 63). The plants must be kept in the shade. If bottom heating is available, it can be helpful in producing rooting. The temperature should be 23°C (73°F). Continue spraying with fungicide once a week, i.e., the container taken out of its cover, sprayed, allowed to drain, and then put back again.

10. The cuttings will root in about four to five weeks and it is usually obvious which have been successful. Tug gently on the cutting and if there is resistance roots have formed.

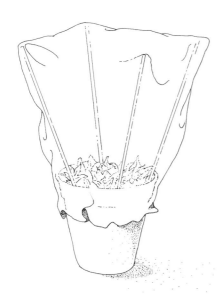

Figure 63. Keep the leaves of cuttings away from a polythene cover by using small canes as supports

PLATE 134. The powerful clematis 'Little Nell' climbs high into rose 'Compassion'.

11. A little air can now be allowed to the plants and increased each day until, in a few days, the cover is taken off.

12. After a further two to three weeks, plant out into 4in. (10cm.) pots, using a suitable potting mixture. Pinch or nip out any central growth to encourage side shoots. Cover for one to two hours a day and then, after a few more days, remove the cover. Continue to spray with fungicide every week.

13. If good growth is made, the plants can be planted in the next largest pot. Again, pinch out central growth to encourage side growth. Keep spraying with fungicide once a week. Give liquid fertilizer once a week.

14. The plants can be planted out in the following spring or can be kept for a further year in a pot. By now you are admiring the hard work of a nurseryman!

Hard Wood Cuttings

This method applies particularly to strong growing clematis such as the Montanas, the Herbaceous Clematis and the Late Species.

The hardwood cuttings should be taken in late winter or early spring.

The end of an inter-nodal cutting should be bruised or wounded by taking a sliver off the bottom. The cutting should be about 4in. (10cm.) long.

The procedure thereafter is as for soft wood cuttings. Heat is not required. If successful the cuttings can be 'potted up' in early summer into 4in. (10cm.) pots. They may be ready for the garden by the autumn or kept in larger pots in a protected area until the spring.

Seeds

The seed or achene of the clematis consists of a base containing the seed and a tail of silky hairs which helps dispersal by the wind.

In Small Flowered Clematis some will produce worthwhile seedlings. The new plant will resemble the parent plant but may be poorer although a few may be better.

Seed from the Large Flowered Clematis will not resemble the parent at all. It is a gamble germinating them as a very large number are likely to be worthless. Occasionally a worthwhile plant will issue but very rarely will a plant be commercially viable.

Select the seed from good plants. The seeds from the Early Clematis may be ready by midsummer and can be used then. The seeds of the Late Flowering Clematis are best kept until the following spring. If they are stored they should be kept in a cotton bag, labelled and put into a refrigerator where they can be chilled below 40°F (4°C) but not frozen.

The seed will germinate in a seed medium in seed pans. Prick out as soon as the seedlings can be handled and put into a soil based compost.

Seeds of the Small Flowered Clematis will usually germinate quickly and produce seedlings in one season.

Seeds of the Large Flowered Clematis may be very slow in germinating and may take up to three years.

Seedlings are potted up into small pots, 'potted on' to larger ones, and in two to three years may produce a bloom.

Chance Seedlings

When hoeing keep an eye out for the chance seedlings of clematis. The seedlings may have come from a nearby plant or from a cross between two of your clematis in the garden. Most of the seedlings will be worthless even though unique. To be worthwhile a new plant must display characteristics not yet available in an existing plant. However, some well known clematis have come about in this way such as 'Margaret Hunt', 'Louise Rowe' and *C. montana* 'Freda'.

Seedlings are 'potted up' as described earlier.

Hybridising

As amateur gardeners have more time than the nurseries, some turn their hand to hybridising and can be very successful at it.

Here an entirely new plant is produced by crossing one plant with another. For those who have the knowledge and the time this is the most exciting aspect of

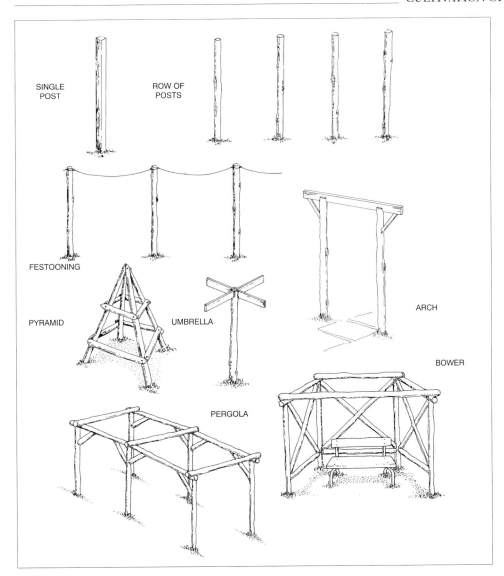

Figure 64. Alternative methods of support for roses and clematis plants

clematis culture. It produces something unique and valuable.

The principles are the same as for hybridising in any genus and any interested reader should consult the specialist literature.

SUPPORTS FOR ROSES AND CLEMATIS

Bedding and Shrub Roses are free-standing and therefore require no support. Here we will discuss the support of Climbing Roses and clematis.

The general idea is to tie the Climbing Roses to supports and then allow the clematis to cling to the roses with their petioles (see Figure 65). The thorns on roses help the clinging although the gardener may wish the clematis to go in a particular direction and so will direct this by using ties.

Additionally, we need to discuss clematis that are not on roses but nearby.

Wood

A simple way of giving support is by the use of posts or poles. These should be used at points in the garden where there is no natural support. Poles can give height to a display of roses or clematis in an herbaceous border. Again, the post with its rose

Figure 65. The rose
entwines the post and
the clematis grows into
the rose

and clematis can be a special feature on a lawn (see Figure 65).

Posts should be of hard wood. They must be buried deep enough into the ground so that they can withstand not only the weight of the rose and clematis but also the stress of the wind. Be sure to coat the post with horticultural wood preservative but not with creosote which is toxic to plants. It is possible to buy a metal base, a spike, which is sunk into the ground or concrete. The post fitting into this has a longer life, is easier to replace, and does not move when under stress (see Figure 67). A post can also be bolted to a surface (see Figure 68).

The rose needs to be tied to the pole and to make this possible the pole should be surrounded by wire netting or wire running vertically.

Usually it is expedient to curl the rose around the post.

Much ingenuity can be employed over the choice of posts (see Figure 64, page 181). For example, it can be just a single post or a row of posts along the length of a border, along the side of a path, at intervals in a shrubbery, or as a partition between one part of the garden and another.

Three posts can be brought together to form a pyramid or tripod so that a rose clings to it and the clematis clings to the rose.

Another interesting way of employing posts is to have an umbrella at the top.

A further attractive way of display is to run a rope, a chain or a wire, between two posts; the rose and clematis is encouraged to run along the support between the two posts thus giving the effect of festooning.

Two posts together joining a third pole make an arch. The arch should be 7-8ft. (2-2.5m.) tall to allow comfortable access when roses are growing on it. Arches can

PLATE 135. Clematis 'Mme Edouard André' clusters around rose 'Compassion' on a
pergola and Viticella 'Minuet' creeps up behind.

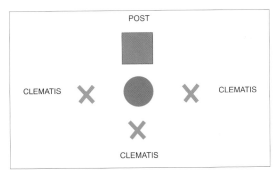

Figure 66. Two or three clematis (x) can be positioned near a
rose (o)

Figure 67. A metal spike

Figure 68. Bolt down
fixing for a post

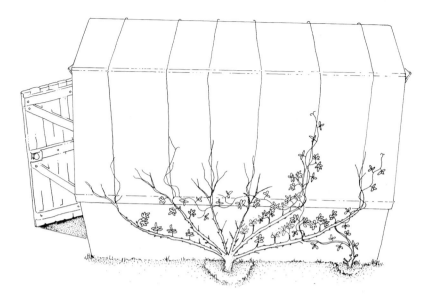

Figure 69. Wire the roof of a shed to encourage a rose such as 'New Dawn' to travel along it. Grow clematis into the rose

make an arbour, bower, gazebo, rotunda or pergola (see Plate 136).

Posts can also be used to make a pergola which can be of simple rustic posts or hardwood.

Each post will usually be able to support one rose and two or three clematis (see Figure 66).

The same principles apply with roses on wooden fences, trellises or screens. There are many types of fences - close boarded, paling, post and rail, post and wire, chain link or interwoven panels.

A trellis should be supported on walls by battens (see Figure 70).

Metal

These metal supports can match all the uses of their wooden counterparts. Single metal structures take the place of a pole or pillar. Combinations of single structures make arches, arbours, pergolas, bowers, gazebos and fences, including chain link fences.

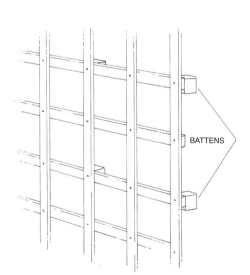

BATTENS

Figure 70. A trellis is fixed to a wall with a batten and offers support to a rose and clematis

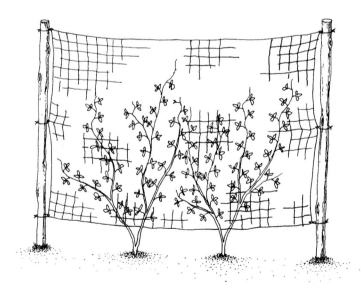

Figure 71. Netting between posts

Stone and brick
Stone structures can match most of the uses of the wooden structures. We can use stone and bricks to make pillars, arches, porches, bowers, pergolas, gazebos, colonnades and, of course, walls.

Walls
Walls can be walls of a house, or a garage, or an outbuilding. They can be walls surrounding a garden or dividing it. Roses and clematis look particularly effective on short walls running down alongside steps.

Roofs
One of the most difficult areas to beautify is the roof of a shed. Wire it in parallel lengths and encourage the roses and clematis to grow along these with sensational results. The roses will give foliage in the winter. The clematis, grown in a sequence, give colour when the roses are not in bloom or match the roses when in bloom (see Figure 69).

Additional support for clematis alone
There will be occasions when clematis are too strong to be allowed to grow with roses and need to be nearby on their own. Useful structures in rose shrubberies are posts, pyramids, and umbrellas near the roses. Some use strong netting hung between two posts up which clematis can climb (see Figure 71).

Training clematis and roses
On walls and fences, where there is sufficient space, Climbing Roses should always be fanned out with the stems as horizontal as possible. Side shoots will grow vertically from these horizontal stems so that ultimately a wall is covered with leaf.

With pillars, the rose may be entwined around it either in a clockwise or anti-clockwise fashion; two or three clematis then cling to the rose (see Figure 65, page 182).

To support roses on walls it is necessary to have strong horizontal wire supports.

The simplest support is a wire running between two nails. It is much better for the nail to be galvanised type or better still a masonry one (see Figure 74). A stronger support comes from using vine eyes driven into the walls at intervals and through which the wire can run (see Figure 72). But the strongest support is given by screw eyes which are screwed to the wall after it has been drilled and plugged (see Figure 73).

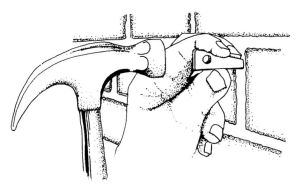

Figure 72. Drive in the vine eye at the junction of the bricks

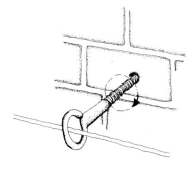

Figure 73. A screw eye supports wire

Figure 74. Masonry nail

PLATE 136. Here we see the modern tendency to use roses and clematis as part of a colourful scene in the garden.

Figure 75. The plastic tie is fixed to the support and left open. The stem is gently placed between the open ends of the ties. The ends are carefully tied together

The wire should be of a gauge strong enough to withstand the weight of the rose, clematis and force of the wind. The wire should be secured at 4ft. (1.2m.) intervals and be 1½ft. (45cm.) apart.

The wire should be at least 2in. (5cm.) away from the wall with the rose tied to it and not to the wall. Thus, when it is necessary to repair or decorate the wall, the ties can be undone and the rose will fall away easily in one piece and lie tidily on the ground.

Tying in Roses

A traditional method is to use pieces of cloth called 'shreds' over the branch of the rose firmly nailed to the wall.

Another method is to use tarred string or strong twine.

Tying in Clematis

A number of ties can be used.

Raffia can be used, where the tie does not need to be permanent, but it is rather obtrusive.

If the gardener has time, green string can be used which is unobtrusive.

Paper covered with ties can be used with clematis that are going to be hard pruned in the autumn. They are impermanent and can only be used for a year.

Plastic coated wire is permanent and quick to use. It should not be allowed to squeeze the stem too tightly and room must be allowed for growth in the diameter of the stem. The gardener soon becomes adept at using these plastic ties (see Figure 75).

PLATE 137. A plastic covered metal trellis makes an effective method of fixing clematis
Vitacella 'Venosa Violacea; and rose 'Pink Perpétue' against a wall.

ROUND THE YEAR CARE OF ROSES AND CLEMATIS

Much of the programme can be undertaken jointly for roses and clematis.

Midwinter

Check that roses are not loosened by wind or frost. If loosened, stamp soil around the rose and trim its foliage to reduce wind resistance.
Prepare rose and clematis beds to be planted in early spring.
Order tools, peat, manure, fertilisers, chemicals, etc.
Water any plants liable to dry out.
Establish, or bring up to date, a plan showing the location of roses and clematis.

Late winter

Planting of roses is possible in mild districts.
Split Herbaceous Clematis and replant.
Water plants liable to dry out.
Check name labels on all roses and clematis.

Early spring

Plant roses and clematis.
Prune Bedding Roses, Climbing Roses, and clematis.
Weed beds.

Mid spring

Apply general fertiliser to roses and clematis.
Start spraying with compatible insecticides and fungicides against black spot, rust, aphids and clematis wilt. Systemic insecticides and fungicides can be watered into the ground.
Start watering programme.

Late spring

Apply mulch of manure or other suitable material to roses and clematis.
Continue spraying as required.
Take clematis cuttings and layer clematis plants.
Continue watering programme.

Early summer

Continue spraying as required.
Cut rose flowers on long shoots and clematis blooms for house.
Apply second feeding of fertiliser.
Continue watering programme.

Midsummer
'Dead-head' rose bushes.
Cut roses and clematis for the house.
Spray fungicides and insecticides or water in – as required.
Continue watering programme.

Late summer
'Dead-head' rose bushes.
Spray as required.
Cut flowers for house.
Continue watering programme.

Early autumn
'Dead-head' roses.
Prune Rambler Roses.
Gather clematis seed and sow.
Order roses and clematis.
Prepare rose and clematis beds for planting.
Reduce watering when possible.

Mid autumn
Tidy beds.
Finish preparing rose and clematis beds for planting.
Collect clematis seed heads and rose hips for decoration.
Reduce watering programme.

Late autumn
Plant roses and well-established clematis plants.
Cut back long rose stems in areas exposed to the wind.
'Earth up' roses in cold exposed areas.
Protect clematis in cold areas.

Early winter
Finish planting roses when conditions allow.
Plan clematis planting and order plants for early spring.
Water plants liable to dry out.

PLATE 138. Clematis 'Margaret Hunt' provides a glorious column of colour against the striking background of a holly hedge.

PLATE 139. Delicate pink rose 'Gertrude Jekyll' sits happily beside glorious clematis 'Durandii'.

POSTSCRIPT

It may be useful after considering growing roses and clematis in some detail to stand back and list some main principles.

In planning your garden make an assessment of how much time you can give to its care. To this add the time that you need for enjoying the roses and the clematis. You need time to smell *Clematis flammula* and rose 'Zephirine Drouhin'. You need time to cut *C.* × *durandii* and floribunda 'Pink Parfait' for your table. You will want to compare the blooms of *C. texensis* 'Gravetye Beauty' with *C. texensis* 'Sir Trevor Lawrence'. You will want to touch velvety 'Niobe'. You will need time to adjust the growth of *Clematis viticella* 'Alba Luxurians' so that you can see its strange beauty to best effect. If you have insufficient time, plan your garden with lawns, shrubs and trees and make a landscape then slip in the number of roses and clematis that can be cared for in the time available. Another way of being economical of time is to use stone and concrete to make patio after patio. Expensive but economical of time.

Fortunate is the gardener who is able to take over a piece of virgin ground and plan his garden as he would wish. Many find themselves taking over a garden already planned by others. In this event a rather ruthless frame of mind is required to produce your ideal garden. Carefully assess the garden, on a plan if possible. Wait a season to see what is there. Mark those features that cannot be moved, for example, a mature tree. Regard the rest as not only moveable but, if need be, as disposable. The more ruthless the gardener the better the end result.

If collecting all the known roses and clematis is your aim then that is a pleasure of its own but not what most gardeners want to do. Indeed, that sort of collecting is best done most economically by rows and rows of plants in a field.

If time is really short remember you will get more pleasure out of twelve well-selected roses and twelve well-selected clematis than if you are in a frantic rush to look after fifty of each.

For the enthusiastic clematarian there is one sure way of getting to know your clematis – by buying one clematis from each of the twelve groups. Buy one Early Large Flowered Clematis (for example, the beautiful 'Miss Bateman') and one Late Large Flowered Clematis (for example, the lovely 'Victoria'). You will quickly learn the difference between the Early and Late Flowering Large Clematis. Then buy just one plant in each of the ten Small Flowered Groups. You start with one of the Evergreen Group in the winter (for example, the scented clusters of *C. armandii*). For early spring choose one Alpina (for example, the large flowered *C. alpina* 'Frances Rivis'). Almost at once will come your chosen Macropetala (for example, the productive and reliable 'Macropetala'). Your choice of Montana will flower next (for example, *C. montana* 'Freda' with its glowing colour and bronzy foliage). Your chosen Rockery Clematis (for example, the exquisite *C. cartmanii* 'Joe') will flower before the spring is over. Early summer will see your choice of an Herbaceous Clematis in bloom and on your table (for example, the unforgettable *C. × durandii*). Choose just one Viticella, difficult when all are so attractive (for example, the long flowering productive 'Etoile Violette'). Choosing just one of so many lovely Texensis is a problem (a good choice is 'Sir Trevor Lawrence' with his multi-colours). Your one choice from the Orientalis group is easy ('Bill Mackenzie' for a large garden or 'Helios' for a small one). Your last choice takes you into the autumn with the late species. (Give yourself the exceptional joy of 'Triternata Rubro-marginata'). Just twelve clematis! From the twelve you will learn the varied habit, strengths, weaknesses, of each group and where it will fit best into your garden and with your roses.

As you get to know roses and clematis well you may develop an interest in one part of these two enormous subject areas, for example, the English roses or the Texensis Group of clematis. You will perhaps become an expert in that group, able to impart knowledge and help to your fellow gardeners while sharing information with the gardening public through publications.

Pruning of roses and clematis is more difficult to write about than to do. If you are bewildered then help is readily at hand. Consult your nearest specialist rose or clematis nursery.

There is much to do during the plant growing period. If you can undertake tasks outside this period then it will release more time for you at the busy season. As autumn approaches do not retire to the house. Correctly attired you will enjoy undertaking a systematic tidy up of the garden. Start at a given point, go right round the garden until you are back at the starting point. This is also the time for construction work – new walls, paths, posts, etc. When the weather drives you indoors, spend some time on the books. Get to know each clematis group. Make a plan of the garden. Plan new plantings (go out to make the holes if the ground allows). Check all your equipment. Order tools and plants. By early spring you will have an immaculate, well-planned garden and you can face up to your first task with relish – pruning. You will also have time to enjoy your plants.

One of the greatest joys of gardening is to produce a new plant which is unique. In our case here, a rose or a clematis. Hybridising is very time-consuming and this is where amateurs come in as they often have more spare time than professionals. Careful study, by reading or attending a course given by an expert, gives a good start. The aim is to be skilful enough to produce a new plant with good points never seen before. In Large Flowered Clematis we need a new breed of plant free of vulnerability to wilt. We must keep away from using clematis for breeding with *C. lanuginosa* in its genetic make-up. Roses have come a long way with exciting new products and more will come. Clematis still have a long way to go in their development and exciting times are ahead.

If you have the time and the resources you may be the person to give us a planned joint rosarium (a garden for roses) and a clematarium (a garden for clematis). I dream of a sloped garden landscaped with shrubs and trees. The slope allows of flowing, musical water that appears in unexpected rivulets, streams, pools, waterfalls, cascades, and fountains. Turning out of a grotto into a small glade, you gasp at the roses and clematis as they are presented in a different way in each glade with a use of wood, stone, pottery and statuary. Glades can concentrate on rose groups – climbing, shrub, bedding or on a group of clematis. There can be glades with seasonal plantings and the best of informal planning will blend with the formal to make this a garden fit for the King and Queen of the climbers.

PUBLISHER'S NOTE

We wish to remind readers that in order to make the text useful in both hemispheres, plant flowering times, etc., are described in terms of seasons, not months. The following table translates seasons into months for the two hemispheres.

Northern Hemisphere		Southern Hemisphere
Midwinter	= January	= Midsummer
Late winter	= February	= Late summer
Early spring	= March	= Early autumn
Mid spring	= April	= Mid autumn
Late spring	= May	= Late autumn
Early summer	= June	= Early winter
Midsummer	= July	= Midwinter
Late summer	= August	= Late winter
Early autumn	= September	= Early spring
Mid autumn	= October	= Mid spring
Late autumn	= November	= Late spring
Early winter	= December	= Early summer

APPENDIX I
Useful Information for the Reader

Readers will derive immense benefit from joining rose and clematis societies as they will be able to share information with others, gain from society advisory services and obtain up-to-date information from attending meetings and reading society journals. This is an essential step for enthusiasts because, even when not a member, societies will usually respond to an enquiry from a gardener. Knowledge will be gained from visiting rose and clematis collections with many famous and large collections already available for rosarians while others are being established for clematarians. Not to be overlooked is the value of talking to fellow gardeners, especially if they grow roses and clematis together. An excellent source of information is to visit specialist rose and clematis nurseries – usually the best source of supply of plants and societies often keep lists of these.

National Rose Societies
Many countries have a rose society. If there is any difficulty in finding its address then enquiries should be addressed to: The Secretary, World Federation of Rose Societies, The Royal National Rose Society, Chiswell Green, St Albans, Herts., AL2 3NR, UK. Telephone: 01727 850461. Fax: 01727 850360.

National Clematis Societies
These are fewer in number and not as old as the rose societies.
The Japanese Clematis Society is the longest established national society. There is great interest in clematis in Japan, many fine examples having been (and still are) raised there with some of its plants used extensively in hybridising programmes elsewhere. The Society publishes a journal in Japanese and, in addition to the National Societies, there are enthusiastic local groups. The address of the Japanese Society is: Japan Clematis Society, 3-30-35, Shirako, Wako-Shi, Saitama-Ken, 351-01, Japan.

The Swedish Clematis Society was founded round the celebrated Swedish clematarian Magnus Johnson. This enthusiastic society publishes a journal in Swedish. Its address is: Swedish Clematis Society, Laxholmsbacken 114, S-127 42 Skarholmen, Sweden. Telephone: 08/7102180.

The British Clematis Society was founded in 1991 and is a large society with a rapidly growing membership in the United Kingdom and among English speaking clematarians worldwide. It has established a trial ground for clematis and it publishes an internationally orientated journal, **The Clematis,** in English. Its address is: British Clematis Society, Bewick Lodge, 4 Springfield, Lightwater, Surrey, GU18 5XP. Telephone: 01276 476387.

In addition there are enthusiastic groups of clematarians in Germany, Denmark, Holland, France, Russia, Latvia, Estonia, China, Poland, USA, Canada and New Zealand. In time there is likely to be a world federation of clematis societies on the same world model as that for roses.

Rose Collections

Every major country has at least one large collection and often a number of smaller ones. Some are general collections while others specialise in new or old roses. These are in addition to many large private collections, several of which are open to visits by gardeners. Information about rose collections can be obtained from the national rose society concerned from the World Federation of Rose Societies at the address above.

Clematis Collections

These are fewer in number and more recent than the rose collections.

Japan holds the largest collection of clematis with an extensive permanent display at the Tsukuba Botanical Garden at Tsukuba Science City, Tokyo. The Botanic Garden was opened in 1983 and extends to 36 acres.

In 1992 France established a national collection of clematis at the famous Bagatelle Garden in Paris under the auspices of the City of Paris. The present collection of 173 clematis will increase in number and contains a wide range of species and cultivars, as well as conservatory clematis. This garden is open throughout the year and is situated at Avenue de l'Hippodrome, 75116, Paris.

In Germany there is a clematis collection at the Botanical Garden of Dortmund. Address: Botanicher Garten, Dortmund-Brunninghausen, Germany. This garden is open throughout the year.

In Italy the marvellous Villa Taranto at Pallanza on Lake Maggiore holds a small collection of clematis.

The United Kingdom has three national collections of clematis but two are not readily available to the public. A third is open to the public at Treasures of Tenbury, Tenbury Wells, Worcs., WR15 8HZ. Tel: (01584) 810777. In addition to many private collections, a focal point for all clematarians is the beautiful Sissinghurst Garden of the National Trust. The Sissinghurst Castle Garden is situated at Sissinghurst, near Cranbrook, Kent and is open 2nd April-15th October. For visitors passing through London there is an interesting collection held in one of the London squares – Eccleston Square, behind Victoria Station. In Scotland, the Royal Botanic Garden, Edinburgh holds a collection at its main and associated gardens.

In the USA three collections are well-established. 1. A collection was started in 1983 at the Jane Watson Irwin Garden of the New York Botanical Garden, Bronx Park, Bronx, New York. 2. A collection at the United States National Arboretum in Washington 25, DC. 3. An expanding collection at the Chicago Botanic Garden.

In Ireland there is a collection at the National Botanic Garden, Glasnevin, Dublin.

Joint Clematis and Rose Collections

There are a large number of private collections worldwide.

In France the Bagatelle Garden also holds a collection of roses and clematis. For the address see above.

In the United Kingdom an ambitious joint project between the Royal National Rose Society and the British Clematis Society has led to more than 200 clematis growing with roses at the former's garden, St Albans, Hertfordshire. This garden is readily accessible by road as it is situated near the junction of the M1 and M25 motorways. A massive expansion of this garden is planned for the year 2000 when it is hoped to extend the rose and clematis collection as well as to include a clematis display garden. This new garden will be open throughout the year. The address is as follows: The Royal National Rose Society, Chiswell Green, St Albans, Herts., AL2 3NR. Telephone: 01727 850461. The Royal Horticultural Society has a fine collection of roses and clematis at its Hyde Hall branch at Hyde Hall, Rettendon, Chelmsford, Essex, CM3 8ET. Telephone: 01245 400256. The garden is open from March to October. A private collection, open to the public, is at Haddon Hall, Bakewell, Derbyshire, DE45 1LA. Telephone: 01629 812855. It is open 1st April - 30th September. Here there is a magnificent collection of old roses and clematis against the backdrop of a beautiful medieval building.

In Ireland, at Grove Gardens, Fordstown, Kells, County Meath, there is a display of 400 clematis and 500 roses. The garden is only open on the following dates: weekends, 17th March- 31st May and weekdays, 1st June-31st October.

APPENDIX II
Tables

Tables from within the book have been repeated here for ease of reference.

Table I
THE TWELVE CLEMATIS GROUPS

LARGE FLOWERED (TWO GROUPS)	SMALL FLOWERED (TEN SUB-GROUPS)

1. Early Flowering
e.g. 'Nelly Moser'
(Can be subdivided
into colour sections)
	Early Flowering
	1. Evergreen Group
	    e.g. *C. armandii*
	2. Alpina Group
	    e.g. *C. alpina* 'Frances Rivis'
	3. Macropetala Group
	    e.g. *C. macropetala* 'Markham's Pink'
	4. Montana Group
	    e.g. *C. montana* 'Mayleen'
	5. Rockery Group
	    e.g. *C. cartmanii* 'Joe'

2. Late Flowering
e.g. 'Jackmanii'
(Can be subdivided
into colour sections)
	Late Flowering
	6. Herbaceous Group
	    e.g. *C. integrifolia* 'Rosea'
	7. Viticella Group
	    e.g. *C. viticella* 'Mme Julia Correvon'
	8. Texensis Group
	    e.g. *C. texensis* 'Gravetye Beauty'
	9. Orientalis Group
	    e.g. *C. orientalis* 'Bill Mackenzie'
	10. Late Species Group
	    e.g. *C. flammula*

Table II
TABLE OF PRUNING REQUIREMENTS

The pruning requirements of each of the twelve groups of clematis are shown in the following Table. If you know which group your clematis belongs to then the Table will tell you the pruning requirement. The clematis are listed according to approximate time of flowering.

PRUNING REQUIREMENTS OF THE TWELVE CLEMATIS GROUPS		
Group	**Example**	**Pruning**
Evergreen	'Armandii'	No Pruning
Alpina	'Frances Rivis'	No Pruning
Macropetala	'Markhamii'	No Pruning
Montana	'Mayleen'	No Pruning
Rockery	'Marmoraria'	No Pruning
Early Large Flowered	'Nelly Moser'	Light Pruning
Late Large Flowered	'Jackmanii'	Severe Pruning
Herbaceous	*C. integrifolia* 'Rosea'	Severe Pruning
Viticella	'Mme Julia Correvon'	Severe Pruning
Texensis	'Gravetye Beauty'	Severe Pruning
Orientalis	'Bill Mackenzie'	Severe Pruning
Late Species	'Flammula'	Severe Pruning

Table III
THE THREE ROSE GROUPS

GROUP 1.	**Climbing** (Climbing Old and Modern Roses)
	A. **Climbers** e.g. 'Compassion'
	B. **Ramblers** e.g. 'American Pillar'
GROUP 2.	**Shrub** (Old and Modern) e.g. 'Canary Bird'
	(A sub-section is the Spreading Group, e.g. 'Nozomi')
GROUP 3.	**Bedding**
	A. **Hybrid Teas** (Large Flowered Bush), e.g. 'Peace'
	B. **Floribunda** (Cluster Flowered Bush), e.g. 'Queen Elizabeth'
	(There are sub-sections of Miniature Roses, e.g. 'Tom Thumb' and Patio Roses, e.g. 'Anna Ford')

Table IV
SYNCHRONISING GROWING CLEMATIS WITH CLIMBING ROSES

The Table summarises the time of the year when growing Climbing Roses and Clematis together can take place.

Column 1 gives the season of the year.

Column 2 summarises what is happening to the Climbing Rose at a given time.

Column 3 tells what clematis groups are available before the roses bloom. It should be used in combination with Columns 1 and 2

Column 4 lists the clematis available when the roses bloom. It should be used in combination with Columns 1 and 2

Column 5 lists the clematis available after the roses bloom. It should be used in combination with Columns 1 and 2

Column 6 lists the clematis available near the rose. It should be used in combination with Columns 1 and 2

Column 7 lists the clematis available beneath the rose and should be used in combination with Columns 1 and 2.

The time periods given are approximate and are those to be expected in an average year.
In years when there is more heat than expected the flowering of the clematis will be brought forward and the season shortened.
In years when there is more dull weather than usual the flowering of the clematis will be delayed and the season lengthened.

AVAILABILITY OF CLEMATIS FOR CLIMBING ROSES

1 Season	2 Roses	3 Before	4 When	5 After	6 Near	7 Beneath
Early winter	Out of flower				Evergreen	
Mid-winter	Out of flower				Evergreen	
Late winter	Out of flower				Evergreen	
Early spring	Out of flower					
Mid spring	Very early roses in bloom	Alpina Macro-petala				Rockery
Late spring	Early roses in flower	V. Early Flowering Clematis			Montana	
Early summer	Main crop in flower		Early Large Flowered	Early Large Flowered		
Mid-summer	Main crop in flower		Early Large Flowered	Early Large Flowered		Texensis Herbaceous
Late	Repeat flowering in bloom		Viticellas Late Large Flowered	Viticellas Late Large Flowered	Orientalis Late Species	Texensis Herbaceous
Early autumn	Some roses in bloom		Viticellas Late Large Flowered	Viticellas Late Large Flowered	Orientalis Late Species	Texensis Herbaceous
Mid autumn	A few in bloom				Late Species	
Late	A few in bloom				Late Species	

INDEX

Page numbers in **bold** refer to illustrations

ANTIQUE COLLECTORS' CLUB

The Antique Collectors' Club was formed in 1966 and quickly grew to a five figure membership spread throughout the world. It publishes the only independently run monthly antiques magazine, *Antique Collecting*, which caters for those collectors who are interested in widening their knowledge of antiques, both by greater awareness of quality and by discussion of the factors which influence the price that is likely to be asked. The Antique Collectors' Club pioneered the provision of information on prices for collectors and the magazine still leads in the provision of detailed articles on a variety of subjects.

It was in response to the enormous demand for information on 'what to pay' that the Price Guide Series was introduced in 1968 with the first edition of *The Price Guide to Antique Furniture* (completely revised 1978 and 1989), a book which broke new ground by illustrating the more common types of antique furniture, the sort that collectors could buy in shops and at auctions rather than the rare museum pieces which had previously been used (and still to a large extent are used) to make up the limited amount of illustrations in books published by commercial publishers. Many other price guides have followed, all copiously illustrated, and greatly appreciated by collectors for the valuable information they contain, quite apart from prices. The Price Guide Series heralded the publication of many standard works of reference on art and antiques. *The Dictionary of British Art* (now in six volumes), *The Pictorial Dictionary of British 19th Century Furniture Design*, *Oak Furniture* and *Early English Clocks* were followed by many deeply researched reference works such as *The Directory of Gold and Silversmiths*, providing new information. Many of these books are now accepted as the standard work of reference on their subject.

The Antique Collectors' Club has widened its list to include books on gardens and architecture. All the Club's publications are available through bookshops world-wide and a full catalogue of all these titles is available free of charge from the addresses below.

Club membership, open to all collectors, costs little. Members receive free of charge *Antique Collecting*, the Club's magazine (published ten times a year), which contains well-illustrated articles dealing with the practical aspects of collecting not normally dealt with by magazines. Prices, features of value, investment potential, fakes and forgeries are all given prominence in the magazine.

Among other facilities available to members are private buying and selling facilities, the longest list of 'For Sales' of any antiques magazine, an annual ceramics conference and the opportunity to meet other collectors at their local antique collectors' clubs. There are over eighty in Britain and more than a dozen overseas. Members may also buy the Club's publications at special pre-publication prices.

As its motto implies, the Club is an organisation designed to help collectors get the most out of their hobby: it is informal and friendly and gives enormous enjoyment to all concerned.

For Collectors — By Collectors — About Collecting

ANTIQUE COLLECTORS' CLUB
5 Church Street, Woodbridge Suffolk IP12 1DS, UK
Tel: 01394 385501 Fax: 01394 384434
—— or ——
Market Street Industrial Park, Wappingers' Falls, NY 12590, USA
Tel: 914 297 0003 Fax: 914 297 0068